INA VERSTL
ERNST FALTERMEIER

THE BEER MONOPOLY

How brewers bought and built for world domination

BRAUWELT
INTERNATIONAL

This book is a publication of
BRAUWELT International
Andernacher Strasse 33 a
90411 Nuremberg · Germany

www.brauweltinternational.com
BRAUWELT International is an imprint of Fachverlag Hans Carl

First published 2016

Photographs
Hilda Lobinger and Liebenow Fotografie

Front cover design by Cornelie Müller
Design by Büro für Angelegenheiten · www.angelegenheiten.de

Printed in Germany on acid-free paper
by Silber Druck oHG · Niestetal

ISBN: 978-3-418-00916-2

CONTENTS

DEDICATED TO RÜDIGER RUOSS

Networker extraordinaire · Founder and President
World Beer and Drinks Forum in Munich

ACKNOWLEDGEMENTS

This book is the result of true teamwork. Individual chapters cannot be assigned to any one of us, since we both contributed to each one.

We owe a debt of gratitude to the French beer economist Germain Hansmaennel, whose Beer World Monopoly provided us with a model to think about globalisation in a wider context. Our many discussions with him over the course of writing this book helped us formulate our argument. His input into this book is far greater than can be expressed in words.

Over the years we have also benefitted greatly from talks with numerous executives and industry insiders. Our heartfelt thanks go to those we cannot name.

Among those we can, we want to single out for gratitude Theo Baal, Owen Barstow, Dr Tim Cooper and Nick Sterenberg, Wolfgang Drechsler, Dr Evan Evans, Björn Falkeström, Dr Karl-Ullrich Heyse, Lyn Kruger and Keith Lemcke, Charles A. Landsmann, Silvia Liebrich, His Royal Highness Prince Luitpold of Bavaria, Charlie Papazian, Wolfgang Riepl, Tullio Zangrando and Omri Zilberman.

Our thanks go to the many organisers of brewers' conferences around the world, who gave us the opportunity to present our ideas, above all Prof. Guido Aerts, John Brauer, Mario Delicio, Dr Lothar Ebbertz, Dr Josef Fontaine, Ian Jones and Mike Williams, Jaime Jurado, Dr Terry Kavanagh, Krishan Maudgal, Esko Pajunen, and the late Bill Siebel, who is sorely missed.

For all their generosity in sharing their wisdom, errors of fact or judgement are entirely our own.

Many people nonetheless contributed immensely to our ability to get this book out. We are boundlessly grateful to Michael Schmitt at Brauwelt International for hosting the roundtable discussion and for allowing us to reuse material from previously published work.

A special 'thank you' is owed to John Harvey, our dedicated first reader, to Simon Tuite for his contribution to the writing and editing of this publication, to Rebecca Jimenez and Jonathan Kovacs for their diligence in sorting out the footnotes and to Lyle Frink for coming up with the title. Many thanks also to Cornelie Müller, our designer, whose great skill and efficiency made it possible for us to meet our deadline. We owe each of them more beer than we can ever carry.

Last but not least, we have to thank our spouses Gabriele Faltermeier and Ernst Hebeker, without whose support this book would never have been finished, and Rüdiger Ruoss without whom this book would never have been begun.

INTRODUCTION

While it is often said of a book that it has been a long time in coming, this is never more true than for this one; ours has in fact been in the pipeline for about a decade. At various times we have commented on the heady dealmaking that has been the dominant feature of the globalisation of the brewing industry, but have ultimately always refrained from publishing our thoughts. We feared that the window of opportunity for our book to make its appearance between two mega-deals would be brief. In fact, we had to wait until the endgame in the globalisation of the brewing industry, which was heralded in 2015 when the world's number one brewer, AB-InBev, made an offer for the world's number two, SABMiller.

With the disappearance of SABMiller the era of globalisation will be nearly over, simply because there are hardly any blank spots left in the world of beer where a heavyweight beer champion has not made its mark. All the major brewing companies appear to have settled into their seats, namely their dominant positions in their respective markets around the world.

Obviously, dealmaking in the brewing industry will continue as the spade of high-profile craft beer acquisitions in 2015 underlines. However, we forecast that on the global scene there will be a bit of a lull, which we hope will be long enough to prevent our observations from being overtaken by major events in the immediate future.

This book is called *The Beer Monopoly* in acknowledgement of Germain Hansmaennel's theory of the Beer World Monopoly which argues that there are certain analogies between the well-known Monopoly board game and the globalisation of the brewing industry. Whoever buys certain streets (i.e. gains market dominance in certain markets), and whoever builds hotels (i.e. brands) has the best chance of erecting an empire which spans the globe.

Being an expert Monopoly player, he confidently predicted in 2006 that the globalisation of the brewing industry had reached the semi-finals and that we would next witness several mega-mergers. Two leading trans-continental groups – InBev (the precursor of AB-InBev) and SABMiller – would be fighting over the lead position. As he said: 'US brewer Anheuser-Busch, as well as the European brewers Heineken, Carlsberg and Scottish & Newcastle, are lagging behind by a large margin because they have stuck to their original markets. I am sure that SABMiller will be a finalist because the South Africans have grasped the rules of the game sooner than their competitors. ... The other finalist will be the brewer who takes over Anheuser-Busch – InBev or Heineken. Without a large-scale takeover, no single brewer can obtain critical mass in the beer business worldwide which is in excess of 20 percent of the global market share. ... On the other hand, there is also the possibility that the CEOs of SABMiller and InBev will agree to merge their companies. In this case there will be no final match but a friendly game of InBev/SABMiller against the rest of the world.'[1] His prognosis proved astute. In 2008 InBev bought the US brewer Anheuser-Busch and set its eyes on acquiring SABMiller.

By calling our book *The Beer Monopoly* we advance the argument that it was through dealmaking and by following the roadmap outlined in Mr Hansmaennel's model that several groups became global players. As these costly acquisitions needed outside financing, the globalisation of the brewing industry fundamentally revolved around money. After each deal brewers had to deliver, meaning they had to produce consistent, dramatic upsurges in profitability.

Of course, there were rival models, such as the often-extolled tactic that brewers need to buy into politically stable markets with low per-capita beer consumption, a youthful population, growing GDP and few competitors, and they would reap the benefits of rising beer consumption.[2] But, in our opinion, this only applies to emerging markets and cannot explain why brewers in mature markets with flat or even declining beer consumption became takeover targets too.

While Mr Hansmaennel's strategy model lies at the heart of our analyses, it was only a means to an end: empire building. Our slogan, 'buy and build', captures the essence of globalisation. It proved a quicker and more profitable route to empires than the old strategy of 'build and brew' (also known as the Heineken Model), which characterised the previous era of internationalisation, and which in turn had superseded beer exports. The term 'build' appears in both, but its meaning has changed. When going 'international' brewers literally built a brewery and started selling locally produced beer. When going 'global' their goal was to build empires, with one takeover being the precondition for the next. It was SABMiller's late CEO Graham Mackay who pointed out that transactions needed to create 'more value' than merely demonstrating 1+1=2. Our formula for dealmaking, 1+1=3, reflects this principle. Sizeable profit growth was the main trajectory as the whole 'buy and build' process followed a deeper rationale, whereby successful deals would help fund the next transaction. It was through taking on and paying down debt that brewers turned themselves into global groups and reliable debtors, thus making their investors very happy indeed.

The rapid globalisation of the brewing industry from the 1990s onwards benefitted from two external factors: politics and finance capital. It was the liberalisation of markets and a world awash with money that helped kick-start the takeover frenzy. What helped too was an industry-specific feature: precisely demarcated territories. Unlike other industries, for example soft drinks and spirits, which revolve around brands, the brewing industry tended to deal in national markets, each with their own players, dominant brands and beer styles, which were the manifestations of their respective beer cultures. This particular feature played into the hands of acquisitive brewers. If they bought the leading brewer in a country, they controlled that market.

Our analyses of the top four global brewers are preceded by a chapter which looks in some detail at dealmaking in the brewing industry since the early 1990s. As there are, and have been, many players in Beer Monopoly, we have included a useful reference list of them at the back of the book. In this chapter we will explain the principles of Mr Hansmaennel's empirical model in contrast with the

Monopoly board game. The differences are significant, most evidently when it comes to winning. The board game only has one winner, whereas the Beer Monopoly has several – meaning several empires. There were also different ways to play Beer Monopoly successfully. You could play it to become number two worldwide or to realise a lucrative sale. You could even play it so that you stalled a rival.

Globalisation began in earnest when brewers did trans-continental deals. The first such deal was Belgium's brewer Interbrew buying the Canadian brewer Labatt in 1995. This transaction marks the game-changer, although export-driven strategies persist to this day.

In the end, though, dealmaking proved a faster path to profit growth than any hike in beer sales could have accomplished. In 1990, US brewer Anheuser-Busch was the world's major brewer, although focused on its home turf, with an output of 108 million hl beer and a profit of $2.1 billion. In 2015, AB-InBev's volume was almost four times larger (410 million hl beer), yet its profit eight times bigger ($16.8 billion), which goes to show that raw size (Anheuser-Busch in the 1990s) is not the same as global clout … or longevity, for that matter.

For investors the growth in the financial numbers alone has been enough to give brewers the thumbs up. By following the beer drinkers and buying into profitable markets, both mature and emerging, brewers managed to grow their bottom lines and succeeded in driving up their share prices. This is reflected in their market capitalisations – the total dollar market value of all of a company's outstanding shares. In 1990 Anheuser-Busch's market capitalisation was $14.4 billion,[3] a modest figure compared with AB-InBev's $200 billion (September 2016). Increasing the share price was clearly of great interest to shareholders. But it was even more important to the brewers themselves. They became predators rather than prey and could afford to clinch deals that were often deemed excessively expensive.

When discussing the top four global brewers we will also examine how dealmaking affected their respective cultures and mindsets. AB-InBev's climb to the top was achieved through 'building positions in the most important beer profit pools in the world', as well as taking a 'disciplined approach to cost management and efficiency' thus 'giving it a strong track record of industry-leading margins and cash flow generation'.[4] Once it stopped being exclusively 'volume-driven' (growing beer sales, that is) and became 'finance-led' (a regime of accumulation dominated by financial valuations), in the words of analysts, AB-InBev revolutionised the industry's *raison d'être*. The most visible effect of this sea-change is the brewers' ranking. In the past companies and markets were ranked according to beer volumes produced. No longer. Because AB-InBev set new standards, the league table for investors nowadays measures companies' profits and countries' profit pools.

In the past century, brewers took great pride in the volumes of beer they produced, as if they rendered a public service by quenching customers' thirst. They strove to be profitable too, but this would have been a secondary consideration to their main objective: raising their beer sales and outperforming their rivals. As soon as they all became stock market-listed companies and had to dance to the tune of investors, business objectives were turned upside down. It became dollars over hectolitres, especially since it was cash and debt that fuelled their chequebook strategies.

Despite its imminent disappearance, SABMiller is given its own chapter because the South Africans' strategy culminated in the most profitable exit in the history of the brewing industry. To secure a high price in the final sale, SABMiller proved a skilful dealmaker. Whereas most of its rivals strove to protect some sort of cultural hegemony (the Brazilians at AB-InBev, the Dutch at Heineken, the Danish at Carlsberg), SABMiller's top management mastered the fine art of keeping large shareholders with diverse cultures and targets in line. Not only did the flexibility that they displayed in this help stabilise the fragile ownership structure, it allowed them to shape and control their own destiny to the very end. Unlike SABMiller, the next-ranking Heineken and Carlsberg are well-protected from being taken over. Heineken has repeatedly stated its desire to remain independent. Among the world's leading brewers it sticks out not least because it is one of the few still in the hands of the founding family – an achievement that is an act of courage and ingenuity. Similarly, Carlsberg has a clear shareholder structure (it is owned by the Carlsberg Foundation) to defend itself from unwanted attention.

Although Heineken was the first brewer to seriously engage in beer exports, it came to globalisation late, probably due to its excessive prudence and risk aversion, characteristics often found in family companies with chequered histories.

Under the circumstances, Heineken has navigated globalisation well. While managing to maintain the family's control and culture, it rejigged its outlook, extracted itself from constricting partnerships and clinched a few formative deals. As a reward it will move up to number two slot in the global brewers' ranking once SABMiller is no more.

Like Heineken, the global number four brewer, Carlsberg, was a late participant in Beer Monopoly. The Danish only joined the club of the big brewers when they entered into a joint venture with Norway's Orkla in 2000. Drawn into the thriving eastern European beer markets, Carlsberg developed a mission to become the fastest-growing brewer worldwide. Yet the decline of the Russian and the Chinese markets has hit Carlsberg hard, both in terms of bottom-line and self-esteem. Controlled by its Foundation and shy to grow through partnerships, Carlsberg may have maintained its Danish corporate culture, yet business-wise it presently finds itself in an impasse.

If we focus on the top four brewers that's because our methodological approach to dealmaking has revealed that among the top four brewers only AB-InBev and SABMiller managed to play Beer Monopoly to its fullest potential. Given the restrictions imposed by their major shareholders Heineken was forced to embark on a catch-up course while Carlsberg had to combine incompatible globalisation strategies. All the brewers further down the ladder, like Japan's Asahi and Kirin, North America's Molson Coors and Turkey's Efes, have been bit-players, in our view, unwilling or unable to follow the rules of the Beer Monopoly.

In going through this book readers cannot fail to notice that certain seminal transactions crop up in several chapters. This is deliberate. Individual motivations varied to such an extent that we felt it necessary to look at them from a number of different perspectives.

To make this book more accessible, we have refrained from using a lot of financial jargon. However, there are a few business metrics that general readers will need to familiarise themselves with, such as profits, profit pool, market share and volumes.

Focusing on cash elements is a response to businesses being finance-led these days. 'Cash flow and profits are brewers' new bedfellows', is something that even Scottish punk brewers BrewDog are keen to stress.[5] Brewers' yardsticks are total EBITDA and profit margins. We use profits either synonymously with EBITDA (Earnings Before Interest, Taxes, Depreciation and Amortisation), or EBIT (Earnings Before Interest and Taxes), which are the internationally accepted standardised means for comparing companies' earnings. Another important and closely related measure is the size of the beer profit pool. Usually given in EBIT, it is an estimate of the total profits earned by all brewers in one market. Not included in the profit pool are the distributors' and the on-trade's profits. For the reason that brewers' market shares based on profits are hard to guess, we use market shares by volume – the percentage share a player holds of total beer volumes sold — instead. Nevertheless, since beer is profit coupled with volume – in 2000, incidentally, it was still 'beer is volume with profit' according to an annual report by Miller Brewing Company — we will give hectolitres (1 hectolitre – hl – is 100 litres) where necessary.

Although we have conscientiously followed the money, this book is not primarily aimed at investors. Our journalistic approach to evaluating brewers' aptitude at playing Beer Monopoly forced us to look backwards because only by assessing their earlier manoeuvres and taking into account formative events in companies' histories will corporate behaviour begin to make sense. Investors, on the other hand, are only interested in the future, more precisely in financial models that will help them predict brewers' prospective growth, profits and share price developments.

Since this is not a book about beer, perhaps we should come clean at this point and state that this is not a book about craft brewing either. The explanation for this omission is straightforward. Craft brewers have not played a role in the Beer Monopoly yet. The stress is on 'yet'. That's why we devote the final part of our book to craft brewers, consumers and politics since they are the three major disrupters in the game and a serious threat to the big brewers.

We readily admit that the Monopoly game can only go so far in explaining the reckless dealmaking in the brewing industry. The board game is finished as soon as there is a clear winner who has driven all his rivals into bankruptcy, while the Beer Monopoly is far more complex since it takes market realities into account. As such it does not allow for closure or a single winner. Our market economies are based on competition, which necessitates at least two players. Undoubtedly, dealmaking will continue, even if only to help the big brewers pay down debts from past acquisitions. It's equally beyond doubt that dealmaking can continue when Mr Hansmaennel's roadmap has run its course and there is nothing meaningful left to buy in beer. It is in recognition of this difference that our book does not have a Conclusion. Rather, we have included our round-table discussion, which covers a range of issues, not least our musings on what the next round of empire building might look like.

BEER GOES GLOBAL, OR THE NEW RULES OF ATTRACTION

"We will be the world's beer company", August Busch III, the President of Anheuser-Busch, predicted in 1996. Twelve years later, Anheuser-Busch was no more. The King of Beer got taken over by a Brazilian-Belgian go-getter called InBev, which had only been formed four years previously. Was Mr Busch's ill-judged prophecy a case of 'pride goes before a fall'? Or had he not seen the writing on the wall, which spelt 'do lunch or be lunch'? August III was an extremely competent corporate chieftain, which his son and successor August IV was not. Both Buschs proved blinkered. While they kept gazing at the US from their executive suites in St Louis, the world of beer was changing beyond recognition. Those who took part in globalisation and its flurry of mergers and acquisitions survived. Those who only reluctantly did so – like Anheuser-Busch – ended up as prey.

Globalisation – in words and deeds – has been with us for so long that few can remember when it all started in the brewing industry. Was it in the late-1970s, when several western brewers entered China through joint ventures that eventually proved doomed? Or was it in the 1980s when two swashbuckling Australian brewers dreamt up the madcap plan to conquer the world by acquiring breweries in Canada, the US and the UK? Or did it only begin in earnest in 1991 when a few determined Finns and Swedes crossed the Baltic Sea to Estonia to take over a state-owned brewery, Saku, that had been advertised as up for privatisation? Could they perhaps have been beaten to the title of first mover by an Australian of the name of Tony Oates who arrived in the Polish port of Gdansk in

1990 to buy some run-down breweries, and whose new beer label, EB, would become the most popular brand in Poland within a few years? Or would that title have to go to Belgium's Interbrew, which in 1995 purchased the Canadian brewer Labatt?

Before memories fade, it is time to lean back in the chair, stare into the embers, and tell the story. And what a story it is. The plot is thick with brash Yankees, boisterous Aussies, soft-spoken Scandinavians, laddish Icelanders, hardboiled Brazilians, pussyfooting Mexicans, no-fuss South Africans, fun-seeking Belgians, dithering Dutch, plus a few clueless Germans and Brits in supporting roles who quickly shunted themselves to the sidelines. All of them had a go at mergers and acquisitions because they came to realise this was the best way to create more value for their companies. As in all good stories, there have been winners and losers, there were chancers and also-rans. And there was what the military calls collateral damage – secondary casualties, but casualties nonetheless.

Of course, all industries that went global in the past two decades have had their fair share of blunders and rookie mistakes, usually made by people who were over-confident but under-informed, not least about cultural differences, thus miscalculating the time horizon needed and the risks involved. But few other industries had such infamous yet colourful characters who hammed it up centre stage with the limelight fully on them. Admittedly, none were a match for August Busch III, the Machiavellian operator who coldbloodedly ousted his father Gussie in a 1975 boardroom putsch and stabbed his own son in the back during the InBev takeover.[1] But in terms of serviceable yet likeable villains, the asset-stripper and convicted fraudster Alan Bond – who became the world's fifth-ranking brewer in 1987 – would be a close second.

If this were a novel, any good editor would send the manuscript back to the author with the comment: 'Overdone, overworked, too many protagonists for the reader to keep track of. Needs major revisions.' But this is not a piece of fiction. It is how the brewing industry came to look the way it does today. In 1990, the top four brewing companies controlled only 25 percent of global beer production. This may seem a lot, until you take into account the fact that three of the four brewers – Anheuser-Busch, Miller and Kirin – sold their beers mostly in their respective domestic markets. But after several gobsmacking transactions between 2000 and 2014, the top four's share had risen to nearly 50 percent.

Doing it the slow way

Even before globalisation became a buzzword, brewers had embarked on a course of internationalising their sales through direct exports. Brewers' early internationalisation stories share several commonalities: location (often near a port) and destination (their countries' historic colonies). Take Bass Ale. By 1870, Bass was the largest brewery in the world, with an annual output of over one million hl beer. Its pale ale, known for its distinctive red triangle on the label, was exported throughout the British Empire. By the 1880s Dutch Amstel, brewed in Amsterdam, was exported to Great Britain and the Dutch East Indies. Early on, these brands competed with the German beer brands Beck's from Bremen and Löwenbräu from Munich. As Germany came to colonies late, her beers drew their international clout and reputation from German brewers' advanced technologies and allowed them to catch up on the lead the other countries had.

So when did internationalisation kick off in earnest? It began with Heineken in 1931 when, together with Fraser & Neave (F&N) of Singapore, a sparkling water company, they set up Malayan Breweries, later to be called Asia Pacific Breweries. Eighty-one years down the road, in 2012, Heineken bought back F&N's stake for $4.6 billion, or at a phenomenally expensive 17 times profits. Back in the 1930s, going it alone was not an issue for Heineken. Sharing the spoils with a local associate proved a profitable undertaking. In the 1930s the Dutch acquired the interests in existing breweries in Egypt, Morocco, the former Dutch East Indies, French Indochina, the Belgian Congo and Palestine. In effect, these deals mark the beginning of Heineken's worldwide expansion.

It was in the 1950s and 1960s that Heineken changed its strategy to 'build and brew' and a series of breweries sprung up in Africa. Changing tack was born out of necessity. Once African countries had gained their independence, they often introduced protectionist taxes, which made imported beers too expensive for the locals. Heineken's only way of response was to enter these markets directly by establishing local breweries. Otherwise they would have lost these markets altogether. Nevertheless, this whole evolutionary process – from exports to build and brew – proved to be a time-consuming strategy, often taking decades to implement. But it came to be known as the Heineken model, and other brewers too adopted this *modus operandi* when seeking to tap into distant markets. Except for Heineken, though, most brewers in the 20th century would have considered beer exports merely pocket money, not their main focus. All the while punters back home were downing their beer in huge quantities, they had better things to do – counting their profits.

We are so used now to hearing Europe's brewers moan about diminishing returns because of supermarket price wars and declining consumption, it is easy to forget that there were times, not so long ago, when brewing was a licence to print money. As recently as the 1970s, a German brewer's business plan was such that all the profits they made from selling mineral water were enough to cover brewing costs. The way they saw it, revenues in brewing equalled profits. Earnings rose even higher when brewers discovered that consumers were willing to pay more for a beer purely on the basis of branding. That is when they began advertising their products as premium beers and turned them into national brands with the help of television advertising. Hence the derogatory term 'TV beers' for large national beer brands. Anheuser-Busch clearly excelled at this because, by branding Budweiser as a premium beer and lifting its price, they increased their market share from 6 percent in 1950 to over 45 percent in 1990 without having to buy a single domestic rival.

Leading Brewing Groups – 1987 (millions of hectolitres)

1	Anheuser-Busch	US	90.1
2	Miller Brewing	US	47.2
3	Heineken	Netherlands	43.0
4	Kirin Group	Japan	30.4
5	Bond Brewing	Australia	29.9
6	Stroh	US	25.8
7	Elders (Forster's)	Australia	21.1
8	BSN (Kronenburg)	France	18.9
9	Coors	US	19.2
10	Brahma	Brazil	18.0

Source: Impact Databank

In 1987 the world's major brewers sold an impressive amount of beer but, except for Heineken and Foster's, this would have only quenched local thirsts. That is because they still had it very easy. In those days, brewers were considered the pillars of their societies. In the English-speaking countries there was even a word for them: 'beerage', a pun on peerage, or 'brewing royalty'. Whether they were called Santo Domingo (Colombia), Fernandez (Mexico), Busch, Coors, Molson, Guinness or Heineken, all believed themselves to be special, a cut above the rest.

However, Britain has always had an ambivalent attitude towards its beerage; a commentator for the *Spectator* magazine wrote in 2008 that this 'cosseted bunch of arrogant monopolists' used their enormous wealth to 'grease the political system, bankrolling the Conservatives who duly obliged by preserving the industry's traditional privileges – including ownership of vast pub estates that sold only the brewer's own beers. What the workers thought of the beerage was clear from the old song: 'I'm the man, the very fat man, who waters the workers' beer,/ And what do I care if it makes them ill,/ If it makes them terribly queer,/ I've got a car and a yacht and an aeroplane,/ And I water the workers' beer.'[2]

The 1980s was a golden time for brewers. In Western Europe, consumption of beer peaked. It stood at 140 litres per head in Germany and Belgium, compared with 120 litres in the UK. There was only one way for it to go: down. The UK brewers had their comeuppance when Australia's corporate raider Elders, at that time the owner of Foster's (Australia) and Courage (UK), launched a hostile bid for Scottish & Newcastle (S&N) in 1988 and the UK's Monopolies and Mergers Commission concluded this was a step too far. It did not just block the deal; it proposed a complete restructuring of the industry under what became known as the Beer Orders. When the UK's brewers were forced by law to dispose of their vast pub estates they decided to turn up their toes and die (or be bought), rather than seek salvation elsewhere.

Go for the money

The 1980s was also the decade of corporate raiders. They were investors who would buy a large number of shares in a stock market-listed company whose assets appeared to be undervalued. By acquiring control, they would then push for changes in the company's leadership, thus increasing share value and generating a massive return for the raider. The first to see that several purely domestic brewers in the UK, Canada and the US proved ripe for the picking were Australia's Elders and Bond. They may have been brewers by name, yet deep down they were raiders.

Extracting all the money they could get from their Australian conglomerates, they went shopping abroad. Putting profits first, the Australians must have taken a long hard look at the global beer profit pool and seen that in these three markets earnings were too good to be left to dithering home-grown brewers. Unlike the family-controlled brewer Heineken, the Australians were not constrained in their ability to raise outside capital to finance their takeovers. In fact, they sought to acquire and build cash-generating businesses in order to provide a steady source of revenue that could be used as collateral for further acquisitions. Seen in this light, other breweries made for almost natural targets.

Taking the rest of the world by surprise, the Australians clinched deals in rapid succession. In 1986 Bond bought Pittsburgh Brewing (US), followed by brewer Heileman (US) in 1987, and took a stake in Allied-Lyons (UK) in 1988. There was speculation that these purchases would not be enough: at an Australian brewers' convention in Brisbane in 1988 there was much agitated talk that Bond would take over Heineken next and then move into China. In similar fashion Elders launched attacks on Courage, England's sixth largest brewer (1986), Carling O'Keefe Breweries, the third largest brewer in Canada (1987), and formed a joint venture with Canada's number two brewer Molson (1989), thus controlling 53 percent of the world's sixth-most-profitable beer market. At some stage in the 1980s Elders also held a one percent stake in Anheuser-Busch and there was speculation that Elders might make a full bid. Failing that, Elders would go after Argentina's brewer Quilmes. Although they had other very ambitious schemes up their sleeves, Bond's and Elders' spending sprees saw them catapulted into the brewers' major league in almost no time.

In the end, these brewing empires unravelled faster than they were put together. Whereas Bond descended into bankruptcy and its remaining Australian beer unit was ignominiously taken over by New Zealanders (Lion), who spoke with a funny accent and used management terms the Australians had never even heard of, Foster's survived, though as a very much pared-down version of its former self, with sales whittled from a high of $15 billion in 1989 to $5 billion in 1994.

Who needs friends if the world beckons

The Australians' ascent may have gone down in management case studies as botched attempts at international acquisitions, but their wheelings and dealings are better understood as 'globalisation – Take 1'. Before everybody else, they saw that the beer business was not about 'making friends' (Gussie Busch's motto), or growing organically. Rather, it became all about making shedloads of cash by stepping outside their home turf and gobbling up other brewers. The Heineken model had outlived itself. It proved far speedier to buy and build, preferably in markets generating a large profit. Lacking that, an assured expanding profit potential would serve just as nicely.

Ironically, although the Australians may have grasped the fundamentals of the game of Beer Monopoly, they came at it too early. They only bought domestic brewers in markets which had not yet fully consolidated into duopolies. Moreover, they did not know how to run these companies so that profits would surge immediately. Because of this managerial failure on top of other mistakes, they ended up drowning in debt.

In the 1980s, the internationalisation of the brewing industry would have been a walk in the park for cash-rich brewers, as bankers of the Gordon Gekko mould (he of 'Wall Street' film fame) would have been more than willing to bankroll them. We should bear in mind that almost all the world's beer is produced in only 40 countries. Thirty years ago, this number was far smaller, as many countries – the ones we like to call emerging markets today – were off-limits to voracious brewers, either because there were political barriers that prevented market entry or because they lay behind the Iron Curtain (all of today's central and eastern Europe). Also, dealmaking would have taken advantage from consolidation in many domestic markets. Except for a few laggards like Germany, the UK and Japan, Western brewers (with a capital W in Cold War speak) operated in markets that were fast becoming duopolies (the US, Canada) or had never been anything but effective monopolies with one company dominating the market (most of Latin America and Africa).

How to play Beer Monopoly

The Beer Monopoly is Mr Hansmaennel's brainchild. He was the first to see that the consolidation and globalisation of the brewing industry resembles the Monopoly game: who buys which streets, i.e. countries, who builds hotels, i.e. brands, who has the best chance to erect a global empire. It took brewers a long time to grasp its fundamentals. A director of a major German brewing company attacked Mr Hansmaennel on stage in front of an audience of 800 people at the World Beer & Drinks Forum in Munich in 2005 by saying: "We do not throw dice!" This man obviously had not figured out that for Mr Hansmaennel the Beer Monopoly only serves as a roadmap, a catchy comparison for the world-wide dealmaking in the brewing industry.

The most successful way to play the traditional Monopoly game is not to aim for the priciest blue streets right from the start. They are the least landed-on squares. Instead, players should try to buy cheapish streets given that squares become more expensive as you go round the board. The point of Monopoly is to own all the streets of one colour. Only then are you allowed to build houses or hotels on them. Like in real life, houses and hotels are in finite supply. Players are therefore best advised to create a housing shortage.

According to Mr Hansmaennel's model, the internationalisation of the brewing industry required aggressive players to first become the leader in their domestic markets: Heineken in the Netherlands through the takeover of Amstel in 1968, Interbrew in Belgium through the merger of Artois and Piedboeuf in 1986, Carlsberg through the 'beer wedding'[3] with Tuborg in 1970, AmBev in Brazil through the merger of Brahma and Antarctica in 1999. Make no mistake; despite the cute choice of phrase – beer wedding being one – it was political goodwill that turned these brewers into money-spinning market leaders in their domestic markets and gave them a head start in Beer Monopoly.

In a next step, brewers had to consolidate their backyards, be they subcontinents (i.e. western and eastern Europe, southern Africa) or continents (i.e. Latin America) to control all the streets of one colour. Whether brewers clinched in-country deals like Heineken in western Europe or pursued a 'build and brew' tactic, as was the case in eastern Europe, is immaterial for this purpose. The attempt to own all neighbouring streets, in Monopoly terms, may smack of 20th century geopolitics. But if we accept that there are such lofty things as cultural realms – best exemplified by the various continental football tournaments – brewers needed to have a full presence in these markets, or the marketing of their international brands would have been pointless. Why sponsor, say, a European event like the UEFA football championship if your brand is not available in viewers' home countries?

In pursuit of a global empire, brewers ideally had to buy both into mature markets because of their nearly failsafe profits, and emerging markets because of their forecasted consumption growth. That way, they minimised their risks associated with emerging markets, such as political and social instability, currency swings, and economic troubles.

However, there is a major difference between the Monopoly game and the Beer Monopoly. It is called cartel. In markets with several players, oligopolies that is, acquisitive brewers are prevented from power shopping because of regulatory barriers. If they are clever they will go after the number one player, not the distant number five. Under a best case scenario, the market leader will enjoy a market share of 30 percent. This is the arbitrary but generally accepted threshold which will make the local antitrust watchdogs prick up their ears but will stop them from baring their teeth. It is accepted wisdom in the brewing industry that you need to control at least a 30 percent market share in order to enjoy the benefits of critical mass, which means good profits and the muscle to set prices. Not enough, any number one player enjoying this sort of market share will have large mainstream beer brands and the concomitant distribution systems, which will form the basis on which the acquirers can place their own so-called 'international lager' brands like Heineken, Budweiser, Stella Artois.

This marks the fundamental difference between beer exports and buying into markets. Lacking a domestic base, international beer brands alone will not accrue the kinds of profits domestic businesses plus international brands will.

As to the aforementioned housing shortage, it should be self-evident that international beer brands with real global appeal are in short supply. Bearing this in mind, AB-InBev's acquisitions were really smart as they went after markets and brands combined. Merging AmBev and Interbrew gave them the Beck's and Stella Artois brands.

Buying Anheuser-Busch landed them with the Budweiser brand. And taking over Mexico's Grupo Modelo presented them with the Corona Extra brand. In terms of global sales, these four brands are already far bigger than their six largest competitor brands in total. What is more, once a brewer 'controls' or 'owns' a country in the manner of the Beer Monopoly and has introduced its own international beer brand, it will have effectively closed off this market to its global competitors. Others will hesitate to break into it. This is why we talk about the Beer Monopoly. Any brewer with a market share in excess of 30 percent per market and a full portfolio of brands – from local brands to international lager – essentially enjoys a dominant position and nearly inexhaustible profits.

Historic windfall

Western European brewers would have had to content themselves with growing their business slowly through exports and licensing agreements plus a few small takeovers, had it not been for a fortuitous political event which brought the Cold War to an end and changed the course of history at the end of the 20th century: The Fall of the Iron Curtain in 1989 and the subsequent collapse of the Soviet Union. For SAB, a few years later, it was the end of apartheid and the lifting of Western sanctions in 1994 which proved auspicious. No longer seen as a backwater brewer, SAB could commence its two decades-long expansion across the globe.

Leading Brewing Groups – 1990 (millions of hectolitres)

1	Anheuser-Busch	US	104.6
2	Miller Brewing	US	62.2
3	Heineken	Netherlands	46.5
4	Kirin Group	Japan	34.6
5	Foster's	Australia	30.5
6	Danone (Kronenbourg)	France	26.5
7	SAB	South Africa	25.8
8	Brahma	Brazil	25.5
9	Guinness	UK	24.3
10	Coors	US	23.7

Source: Impact Databank

In so-called management bibles from the 1990s they gave you all kinds of highfaluting advice on how to become an international player. In actual fact, it was fairly basic stuff. In the case of the brewing industry, it was old-style gun-boat imperialism in many markets, done by men in business suits instead of uniforms. They went out and planted their flag on foreign shores after exchanging pleasantries (and money) with the local chieftain.

Move east

This is not to say that entering into soon-to-be major beer-swilling markets like China and eastern Europe (with a lower-case 'e' in post-Cold War diction) was imperialistic. Although lots of breweries came on the market that sold for a song, buyers had to choose their targets carefully. Especially in central and eastern Europe, the breweries that were put up for sale in privatisation programmes were showing their age. Worse, there were no western-style markets to speak of, as the previous centrally-planned regimes had imploded and 'economic transformation' (the euphemism at the time for the radical switch from a socialist market economy to a free market economy) took its time.

But, looking back on it, adopting a 'build and brew' tactic in chaotic central and eastern Europe was an once-in-a-lifetime opportunity for brewers who took the plunge and learnt that risk-taking can pay off handsomely. With consumers hankering after a beer and a nice brand – not having had either before – foreign brewers only had to rev up production capacity, brew good-quality beers, stick on attractive-looking labels, and the market would be theirs.

Mapping brewers' acquisitions in the 1990s is a near-impossible task because it was a crowded playing field and strategies differed. Perhaps the players themselves did not know if were they in for the long run or only seeking a profitable exit. In those days, the success of a venture and its failure lay close together, depending less on managerial excellence than on external factors and plain luck. What follows is a convoluted narrative of dealmaking intended to counter any false impression among younger readers that the rise of AB-InBev, SABMiller, Heineken and Carlsberg to global brewer status was already a given then, or that they were the only ones intent on playing Beer Monopoly.

The Vikings return

Sneaking behind the Iron Curtain was the opportunity for the daredevils among brewers. That they were the new Vikings from Scandinavia, whose ancestors in the 9th century AD had sailed from the Baltic Sea along rivers into Russia and the Ukraine as far as Constantinople, today Istanbul, should not really come as a surprise. By order of appearance in Russia, there were the three adventurers from Iceland, the twenty-something Bjorgolfur Thor Bjorgolfsson (Thor to his friends), his father, Bjorgolfur Gudmundsson, and Thor's pal Magnus Thorsteinsson. Next came the Swedish brewer Pripps, plus the Finnish brewers Hartwall and Sinebrychoff. The Finns are not strictly speaking Vikings, but why let a minor detail get in the way of a good story?

The Norwegians, Swedes and Finns were the more experienced operators. At least they knew how to make and sell beer, albeit in small quantities – their total market volume was 11 million hl – and in a thoroughly regulated environment. The Icelanders, on the other hand, did not have that experience, but this did not stop them from going to St Petersburg in the early 1990s to found a beverage business. They were opportunists; in polite English, venture capitalists in pursuit of an exit strategy. [4] The Nordic brewers who set up Baltic Beverages Holding (BBH) probably initially thought they would be in it for the long haul. Sadly, it was the ownership split between Swedish-Norwegian Pripps Ringnes (which later went to a Norwegian conglomerate by the name of Orkla, which sold it to Carlsberg) and Finnish Hartwall (who sold themselves to S&N) which eventually proved the demise of BBH in 2008.

Let us begin with the Icelanders. Despite their being seriously underfunded, in 1993 Thor and Magnus, with a helping hand from Thor's father, formed the Baltic Bottling

Plant in St Petersburg. Ownership of that company would later be contested in the courts. Once that got sorted, the Icelanders sold the plant to Pepsi and used the proceeds to move into brewing beer with the launch of Bravo International in 1998. Venturing into brewing was bold – to say the least. For one, the Russian economy was in trouble (the Rouble Crisis) and foreign investment was drying up. For another, St Petersburg was regarded as the capital of the Russian mafia and the drinks sector was seen by the mafia as their target industry of choice, as the UK's *Guardian* newspaper said in 2005.[5] Yet, against all the odds, the Icelanders persevered. Other St Petersburg brewing executives were not so fortunate. According to the *Guardian*, in those wild-wild years, 'Baltika's finance chief was shot dead in his flat through a window. Another perished in a hail of bullets as he stepped from his Mercedes. And one St Petersburg brewery burned to the ground after a mishap with a welding torch.'

Still, in less than three years Bravo was one of Russia's leading brewers, having secured a 17 percent market share in the St Petersburg region and 7 percent in the Moscow area, which were Russia's biggest markets. It was selling 2.5 million hl of beer in 2001 and was heading for 4 million hl when Heineken bought it for $400 million in 2002. Exit the Icelanders as rich men.

Collateral damage

The company founded by the Scandinavians, BBH, was even more of a success, both in terms of volumes and profits. From its beginnings in 1991 with the purchase of an Estonian brewery until Carlsberg took over S&N

together with Heineken to gain full control of BBH in 2008, the investment's value rose to almost $14 billion. In comparison, the original outlay must have been negligible. In a mere decade, from 1991 until 2001, BBH's beer volumes increased from 140,000 hl to 24 million hl, not least thanks to a rapid succession of deals and the quickly growing Russian market, where Baltika Brewery soon became the number one beer company with an output of 14 million hl and a market share of 30 percent (2001).

The rise of BBH must be attributed to a large extent to the Scandinavians' wise decision to leave operations to local managers. The Scandinavians rightly deemed the local barons better suited to handle all that goes on in their back yard. The joint venture between the Norwegians, Swedes and Finns itself worked well because within BBH the Finns occupied a central role as go-betweens. The Finns had a tradition of doing business with the Soviet Union, and were essential in gaining trust from the easterners as well as in convincing the Norwegians and the Swedes that the risks were worth taking, as two academics, Jan Svennevig and Maria Isaksson, concluded in 2006.[6]

Like marriages, joint ventures are made in heaven but need to be micro-managed on earth. Cracks began to appear in BBH's happy-clappy Scandi venture when the partners started differing over strategy and Carlsberg, perhaps out of Scandinavian sibling rivalry, decided that they should not be left out of the party. They made eyes at the Norwegians – Orkla – and the Norwegians threw their lot in with Carlsberg in 2000 to found Carlsberg Breweries. Two years later, in 2002, Hartwall sold itself to S&N for $1.7 billion.[7] At the time many wondered why, as good neighbours, Hartwall did not succumb to an offer by Carlsberg? The answer is, if there had been an offer, it was probably too miserly. Still, Carlsberg got lucky when a frustrated Orkla exited from Carlsberg Breweries in 2004. That meant Carlsberg alone controlled 50 percent of BBH. But when S&N prettied itself up for a sale, Carlsberg worried that it would have to put up with a different partner. So they themselves began shopping around for an accomplice who would help them take over S&N. Fortunately, Heineken proved a willing brother-in-arms. In 2008, S&N was bought and broken up, and Carlsberg became the sole owner of BBH.

What does all the above make BBH? A victim of its owners' quarrels? Collateral damage? In all probability, the latter. Alas, Carlsberg's triumph at BBH was short-lived because in 2009 the Russian economy took a hit and the regulatory environment for brewers turned hostile. Today the Russian beer market is a shadow of its former self as volumes and profits are falling.

Investment fashions come and go

The reason we have charted the Vikings' acquisitions in eastern Europe in some detail is that brewers have always been ardent followers of fashion – or fashion victims, depending on your point of view. Because they had to play to the gallery of investors and bankers, they turned themselves into conglomerates in the 1970s (for example, US brewer Coors owned businesses including ceramics, food products, biotechnology, oil and gas, and health systems, Anheuser-Busch had theme parks, Canada's

Labatt interests in food, dairy and entertainment), only to become focused brewers again in the 1990s when bankers and investors concluded that conglomerates were 'Oh so last season' and decided that it was geographical expansion that would give brewers the wow factor. Twenty years ago, the flavour of the month in investment circles was eastern Europe. Fifteen years ago, it changed to the BRICs (Brazil, Russia, India and China).

In the 1990s, Belgium's Interbrew heard this message well, as did a brewer – SAB – few of us Europeans even knew existed until South African advance parties started popping up all over central and eastern Europe. The countries that lay between Germany's eastern border and Russia were considered burgeoning markets, especially the Czech Republic, where beer consumption exceeded 140 litres per capita. But unlike Poland, whose prospects were even rosier because of its larger population, the Czech Republic benefitted from what international brewers thought they understood best: brands, like Pilsner Urquell. However, before they could lay their hands on it, Pilsner Urquell was snapped up by the Japanese investment bank Nomura.

Like the private equity firm CVC, which bought InBev's central European unit in 2009 for $3.0 billion and sold it to Molson Coors in 2012 for $3.5 billion, Nomura's entry into beer was plainly and simply with a profitable exit in mind. In 1998 they sold the business to SAB, which had outbid the German brewer Krombacher when offering close to $700 million for the Czech breweries Pilsner Urquell and Radegast. To SAB, the beauty of the deal was that not only did they get a business which enjoyed 45 percent of the

Czech market and thus leadership, they also got a brand which had, they believed, international clout.

Hiding out in Poland

In view of the fact that the Czech Republic has for long been a mature beer market (beer production actually declined to 18 million hl in 1999 from 24 million hl in 1991), many brewers chose to pile into Poland instead. Rightly assuming that beer production could only go up, which it did from 12 million hl in 1991 to 20 million hl in 1999, almost everybody headed off to this new Klondike: Carlsberg, SAB, Heineken, the German brewers Binding, Bitburger and Holsten, the Belgian brewer Palm and ... Mr Bond's former general, not his mere lieutenant, as others claim, Tony Oates.

As an opportunist, no one came near Tony Oates. Having been given a cheque to the order of a few million dollars – according to rumours – by a wealthy Australian lawyer, Mr Oates was lucky to head off to Poland just when the Bond empire disappeared into a black hole. In rapid succession he acquired several breweries, which he wrapped up in a company called Brewpole. Thanks to his successfully launching a new beer brand, EB, in 1992, Brewpole rose to become Poland's biggest beer producer in 1998 with a 25 percent market share. Heineken immediately realised that the only way ahead for them in Poland was to combine their interest with Brewpole's. As they say, if you can't beat them, join them. In late-1998 Heineken's brewer Zywiec and Brewpole merged to form Grupa Zywiec through a share swap, with Heineken owning 61 percent.

Unluckily for him, Mr Oates' past caught up with him in the mid-1990s when he was charged with corporate fraud in Australia. Although he managed to prevent his extradition to Australia for seven years, Mr Oates had to return to Australia in 2003, and in 2005 he was jailed for three years and four months after pleading guilty. He is said to have come back to Poland, but nothing has been heard of him since. How much of a cut Mr Oates got from the deal with Heineken we will never find out.

Playing tag, or what?

Seeing that Poland was being fought over by far too many players, Belgium's Interbrew wisely decided to give the market a wide berth. Instead, they spent the 1990s buying breweries elsewhere, always with an eye to obtaining market leadership or, failing that, the number two position. They clinched a deal with the Indian SUN group, which gave them access to Russia. They bought into China and in 1998 they acquired a 50 percent stake in Korea's Oriental Brewery after the Asian Crisis had caused prices to plummet.

On the face of it Oriental was a bad deal because its beer volumes were falling. However, when, in the following year, Oriental bought the Cass beer brand from Jinro-Coors, (a joint-venture between Korea's Jinro and US brewer Coors which had gone bust in 1997), and built it up again, Oriental managed to reclaim market leadership from its rival Hite in 2000. To finish this story: Interbrew's Korean unit must have been a very nice and profitable stand-alone business, because when AB-InBev sought to reduce its debt in 2009 after taking over US brewer

Anheuser-Busch for $53 billion, they sold Oriental to a group of private equity outfits for $1.8 billion. Five years later they bought it back for $5.8 billion.

Oriental would have been a big acquisition for Interbrew. But the one deal which proved a real stepping stone for Interbrew in the 1990s, in the sense that it freed up a massive profit stream and allowed them to set their eyes on multi-billion targets like Bass, Whitbread and Beck's, was with Canada's brewer Labatt in 1995.

In fact, the Labatt takeover proved a game-changer in other respects too. As stated above, it was the first trans-continental transaction between two market leaders. In those days that sort of manoeuvre was considered avant-garde. The takeover of market leaders only became a must in the next decade. While Interbrew's rivals continued to clinch deals on their respective continents, the Labatt transaction heralded a new era. Internationalisation had drawn to a close; globalisation, aka the formation of global companies through 'buy and build', had begun.

Stock market-listed Labatt was vulnerable to shareholder discontent and a hostile takeover, because in 1994 it had paid $510 million for a 22 percent interest in Mexico's number two brewer FEMSA Cerveza, which boasted of such brands as Sol, Tecate and Dos Equis. Labatt's shareholders complained that management had paid too much as at the end of the year the Mexican currency collapsed (the Peso Crisis). They were adamant that Labatt should divest its entertainment holdings – long-promised by management but never delivered. In May 1995 a $1.7 billion hostile takeover offer landed on Labatt's table. Management naturally rejected this offer and looked around for a white knight, a preferred acquirer, to save them.

Along came Belgium's Interbrew with $2.0 billion. Interbrew managed to quickly sell off Labatt's broadcasting businesses for $650 million, but still thought they had paid too much for Labatt. Seeing that FEMSA might turn out a bargain because of its position in the profitable Mexican market, Interbrew shrewdly managed to raise their stake in FEMSA Cerveza to 30 percent. But relations between Interbrew and FEMSA soon hit a rocky patch, more so when Interbrew merged with AmBev in 2004. That is when FEMSA was allowed to buy back this stake for $1.3 billion, valuing FEMSA's beer business at $4.3 billion. Six years later, when Heineken acquired FEMSA, the business' value had jumped to $7.6 billion.

In the 1990s, sources say, Interbrew clinched about 20 deals in 15 markets for some $9 billion. Funding for these transactions would have been drawn from the profitable Belgian market, but eventually it would be replaced by the far more cash generative Labatt. Interbrew's production volumes went from 15 million hl in 1992 to 72.4 million hl in 1999, with the Belgian business accounting for less than 8 percent of the company's total, compared to 43 percent in 1992. By the year 2000, the company had brewing operations in 23 countries, up from only four a decade before.

The eastern Klondike

Those who lived to tell the tale say that the 1990s were outrageous times in the brewing industry. Without making a moral judgement, the conquest of central and eastern European beer markets is best likened to the Alaskan Gold Rush in the late-19th century, when news that a ton of gold had been found in Alaska started a stampede of an estimated 100,000 prospectors. Like the gold diggers, those brewers who went east would have had a grand strategy. But did they also have a plan as to how to?

It is one thing to do a bit of brewer's maths: low per capita consumption times a large population equals potentially huge beer volume increases. It is another to go barnstorming. Fortunately, whatever their plans were, they remained hidden by the fog of war. If they messed up, overpaid, or floundered, it was highly likely few people would take note of it elsewhere. Little wonder that the first decade following the fall of the Iron Curtain was shaped by opportunists. Theirs was the genuine entrepreneurial spirit. Even if they lacked the necessary experience or ability, they allowed themselves to be driven by one basic goal: just go and do.

In those days, everybody flew by the seat of their pants. Be they exit artists or corporate vanguards, no one had a strict navigation plan or any reliable instrumentation when it came to flying into new markets. For those of us on the ground in Europe, the planes flying into Poland made the loudest roar. In fact, Poland became the eastern experimental lab, where investors with dollars and beer in their eyes thought they would develop a strategy for the subsequent takeover of the Russian brewing industry, which promised to be another Poland, but four times bigger. The conquest of the Polish brewing industry by foreign brewers was swift and lucrative. However, little did they know that their blueprint would fail when confronted with Russian realities.

With the benefit of hindsight we can see now that the constant drone from central and eastern Europe blanked out the noise from other parts of the world. That is why, unbeknown to most of us in Europe, the internationalisation of the brewing industry had already proceeded much further. By the end of the 1990s, Africa's 54 countries had been carved up by SAB from South Africa and Castel from France, with Heineken and Diageo/Guinness also holding stakes in a few. The reason they managed to expand their African portfolios so quickly was plainly lack of competition, or rather refusal to engage in competition. Except for perhaps a handful of markets, for most of the 20th century Africa had had one brewer per country. Once international brewers had acquired the local market leader or built a brewery, the market was theirs. Without resorting to a Berlin Conference like the one held in 1884–85, when the then European powers agreed on political divisions and spheres of influence in Africa, the four brewers, seemingly by unspoken agreement, had accepted the 'first come first served' rule. Pierre Castel, whose beer and soft drinks company BGI has a monopoly in most of its 20 African markets, bluntly defended it by saying: "It's better to have an undisputed monopoly than to be weakened by competition."[8]

The richest guy in Colombia

An Italian by the name of Christopher Columbus may have discovered America, but when it comes to the conquest of Latin America, European brewers were conspicuously absent. It would certainly have been less of an effort for them. There are only seven major beer producing countries on this continent. Brazil has always been the biggest market, selling eight times as much beer as Argentina, ranked fourth, or 22 times as much as Ecuador, ranked seventh (figures for 2015). As in Africa, most of Latin America's beer markets were non-problematic and very profitable monopolies, dominated by family-owned conglomerates. Jorge Paulo Lemann, one of the masterminds behind AmBev, has long understood the power of beer to make fortunes. He reportedly said: "I was looking at Latin America and who was the richest guy in Venezuela? A brewer. The richest guy in Colombia? A brewer. The richest in Argentina? A brewer."[9]

Facing practically no domestic competition, these brewers were fairly complacent and easily pushed around. The task of consolidating Latin America fell to the Brazilian AmBev, which was itself the result of a merger of Brazil's two major brewers, Brahma and Antarctica, in 1999.

By 2000, AmBev had entered both Venezuela and Argentina. Intimidated by AmBev's gun-boat approach, Argentina's leading brewer Quilmes soon beat a retreat too and sold out in 2003.

The reason European brewers chose to give Latin America's enormously profitable brewers a berth may have been that in the 1990s they were all busy piling into China, lured by the country's huge potential. China's per capita beer consumption was about 18 litres a year in the 1990s, compared to 84 litres in the United States and 75 litres in western Europe.[10] Approaching China from the coast, they would buy their way into the more affluent eastern and southern provinces. While we pored over maps to find all those megalopolises where investors had acquired stakes in some of China's then 700 or so breweries, the westerners' local outfits chalked up substantial losses. Those shortfalls were usually swept aside with the argument that 'China is our future' and 'The investment will turn profitable in the long-term'. No one knew or would admit that 'long-term' in China's case would mean eons rather than a decade, and that westerners' resilience or hardnosedness would easily be matched by that of the Chinese. Still, those who persevered in China helped raise beer output so quickly that by 2002 China surpassed the US as the world's leading beer producer.

The world is flat

Although it seems exaggerated to say that the new millennium ushered in a new era in the brewing industry, it most definitely did. In 2000, while champagne producers were still totting up their revenues and the rest of us recovered from all the worrying over the Y2K-bug, the world stopped being a globe. As we would soon see for ourselves, it had turned flat and had shrunk from large to medium-sized. The piecemeal land grab had run its course; there were no more markets left to conquer that were undefined or underdeveloped.

Those who knew how to read the signs of the times could easily predict what would follow next. Brewers had to buy up each other to continue growing. In the Noughties the brewing industry turned into a hush-hush marriage market without it ever quite becoming clear to the outsider who would make the overtures, who was willing to succumb, and who preferred to blend into the wallpaper. The brewers' hurly-burly matchmaking could have been straight out of a Jane Austen novel. Everybody was making eyes at everybody, with SABMiller's CEO Graham Mackay proving a real Lothario, while the dowagers (aka the bankers) looked on. But since this matchmaking was conducted in the rarefied air of the executive suites, brewers kept us guessing during their courtships who would have the advantage of choice and who had the power of refusal.

The list of takeovers in the Noughties can still make you giddy. In actual fact, there were only a few formative deals, which gave the acquirer, above all Belgium's Interbrew, a real shot in the arm. Although the Belgians' acquisition of brewers Whitbread and Bass in the UK was hubristically disdainful of the UK's competition watchdog, which eventually tore it apart, it nevertheless triggered a chain reaction. The Belgian owners of Interbrew realised that they had to think even bigger and so approached Brazil's AmBev with a marriage proposal, while the South Africans got the jitters that they might be next on Interbrew's list and sought refuge in proposing to Miller Brewing in the US and the brewer Bavaria in Colombia.

Hello sailor

The motivation of the sellers marked the most significant transition from the Nineties to the Noughties. Whereas previously most sellers would have been driven by fear and would opt for a retreat, on the basis of 'don't twist my arm, I give in', several sellers in the Noughties decided to pretty themselves up for a sale, choosing a strategic exit instead. Luring potential buyers in with a siren song that was starting to sound like 'hello sailor, how about us', individual voices turned into a veritable trans-continental chorus, with Bass and Whitbread, Germany's Beck's, Miller, Austria's BBAG, and Colombia's Bavaria crooning the loudest.

The takeover of Anheuser-Busch by InBev in 2008 would have stuck in people's memory as the highest-profile takeover ever. Yet it was the attempted purchase of UK brewer Bass by the Belgians which determined the course of history, as it would have been the second time in only five years that Interbrew bought a beer market leader in a country with a sizeable profit pool. In the summer of 2000 Interbrew announced they would spend some $4 billion to buy the Whitbread and Bass breweries, demonstrating their commitment to become one of the world's biggest brewers. Flush with money following their $3 billion stock market debut in the same year, they made an unconditional offer for Bass even before regulatory clearance had been gained, probably hoping to outbid all of Bass' other suitors.

Many questioned Interbrew's decision to press ahead with the Bass deal as, combined with Whitbread,

Interbrew's total UK market share would have soared to 38 percent and way above what the anti-trust watchdogs deemed acceptable (30 percent). Imagine how stunned Interbrew's top brass must have been when in January 2001 the UK regulators blocked their acquisition of Bass. Why did the Brits prove so pig-headed? Had not the Belgian authorities waved through the merger of brewers Artois and Piedboeuf, which started the resulting Interbrew company off with a market share in excess of 60 percent? Had not the Brazilian authorities acquiesced when the country's two major brewers, Brahma and Antarctica, did the same and suddenly enjoyed a 70 percent market share? Defiantly, Interbrew appealed against the decision but to no avail. In the end they had to sell some of the Bass portfolio to the US brewer Coors at a loss.

Seemingly undeterred by their British fiasco, Interbrew continued snapping up breweries in Germany in 2001, splashing out a hefty $1.6 billion on the export brewery Beck's. No one at Interbrew has been able to give a convincing explanation as to why they would spend billions of dollars on German breweries over the next couple of years, which only provided them a market share of 10 percent and not much joy ever since. Germany's beer market was very fragmented, in decline, and profits on beer meagre compared to most other European markets.

Well, in early 2001 Interbrew's Dutch rival Heineken had formed a joint venture with another German brewing group, owned by the Schörghuber conglomerate, which Interbrew must have interpreted as meaning that Heineken was planning the large-scale consolidation of the German market. This was not to be. Funnily enough, nothing could have been further from Heineken's minds: they were only interested in the stake Schörghuber indirectly held in the far more profitable Chilean brewer CCU. This stake Heineken acquired in 2003.

Ultimately, the accusations by analysts and investors that Interbrew had paid too much for acquisitions and was too slow in integrating them into the business formed a black cloud over Interbrew's CEO at the time, Hugo Powell, especially as Interbrew's share price was languishing in the doldrums. When Mr Powell took the clearly daft decision to sue British newspapers over publishing leaked documents, which described in detail how Interbrew would take over SAB, codenamed 'Zulu', his fate was sealed.

Deal chatter fells CEO

From the present-day perspective, it is hard to understand how the documents could have caused such uproar and bring a CEO down. The plan to buy SAB may just have been an intellectual exercise in how to do it, but speculating on potential deals has since become a popular pastime among bankers and media hacks. Many years before AB-InBev announced its intention to take over SABMiller, there was public talk over who would buy SABMiller, to the extent that SABMiller's top executives even gave the media a price tag for their company.[11] Back in 2001, Interbrew considered those leaked plans an affront. No doubt, Interbrew buying SAB in 2001 for an assumed consideration of $6.6 billion in a hostile takeover would have been most timely. The deal would have created the world's number two brewer, only marginally smaller than Anheuser-Busch, and would have given Interbrew more exposure to emerging markets.

SAB's response is interesting in this regard. 'SAB Chief Executive Graham Mackay said he was "truly astonished" [!] by the news of the leaked document and had received an apology from Interbrew. He added that SAB did not need a major transforming deal', South African newspapers reported at the time.[12] While feigning ignorance in public, Mr Mackay was already putting together his own deal. He sought to buy the number two brewer in the US, Miller, which its owner, the cigarette company Philip Morris, had quietly put up for sale. The takeover, sealed in 2002, turned SAB into SABMiller and made the new company too expensive for Interbrew to swallow.

With SAB temporarily struck off their list, the Belgian majority owners of Interbrew took matters into their own hands and secretly began working on a transaction with the Brazilian owners of AmBev, even cutting out their own CEO, John Brock, from the negotiations. Mr Brock was only put into the picture a few weeks before the announcement was made in 2004, as Wolfgang Riepl writes in his book, *De Belgische bierbaronnen* (The Belgian Beer Barons).[13] The combination between Interbrew and AmBev to create InBev in 2004 would mark the second major trans-continental deal in the Noughties after SAB's tie-up with Miller. But this one had more far-reaching consequences. Geographically, the new InBev was only two steps away from controlling the most profitable single-colour streets in the game of Beer Monopoly. Already in a commanding position in most of Latin America and Canada, it only lacked a US and a Mexican brewer. This matter was taken care of when InBev bought Anheuser-Busch in 2008 and took over the rest of Mexico's Grupo Modelo (Anheuser-Busch owned a 50 percent stake in Modelo) in 2013. As soon as they had the Americas under their belt, the re-named AB-InBev could set its sight on taking over SABMiller.

The rest of the story is quickly told. Once InBev was established the hapless Mr Brock was ousted and replaced by the Brazilian Carlos Brito, who had been his chosen heir all along as far as the Brazilian shareholders were concerned. At their behest, Mr Brito rolled up Anheuser-Busch, Modelo and now SABMiller, to become the world's biggest brewer by a wide margin to second-ranked Heineken. All in all, it took the Belgians and the Brazilians barely two decades to accomplish their mission.

Next exit: Edinburgh

The mission the UK's brewer Scottish & Newcastle (S&N) pursued was far shorter but no less clever. Theirs would become the most successful exit strategy in the brewing industry in the Noughties, although ultimately outshone by SABMiller's exit this decade. Back in 2000, S&N ranked 21st among the world's major brewers. No one would have rated their chances of becoming a brewing industry heavyweight high, since they did not even own the brands that were their biggest sellers in the UK: Kronenbourg's 1664 and Foster's. Perhaps to rectify these matters, in 2000 they began expanding outside the UK via the purchase of the French brewer Kronenbourg, which its owner, Danone, had thrown onto the market at a fairly inflated price. S&N did not mind overpaying as they would next buy the Finnish beverage company Hartwall in 2002. The small Finnish market was a side-issue, because Hartwall's most valuable asset was the 50 percent stake in BBH, which encompassed the highly profitable Russian brewery Baltika.

While Carlsberg must have been seething with rage, S&N went on to acquire stakes in the Indian brewer United Breweries in 2002, the Portuguese brewer Unicer and China's Chongqing in 2003. In 2006 they bought the rights to the Foster's brand in Europe in perpetuity. By 2008, when S&N was sold, the company had mopped up an assortment of businesses, which provided neither synergies nor huge profit streams, except for Kronenbourg. However, Carlsberg desperately wanted S&N's stake in BBH. They persuaded Heineken to join them in a deal to take over S&N and break it up between them. S&N played its cards so well that Carlsberg and Heineken had to raise their offer three times, driving their own shares lower because of concerns they would overpay. In the end, S&N sold for USD $15.4 billion. That was phenomenally expensive in relation to what the buyers got. Heineken ended up with a UK business that would turn out to be a can of worms and an Indian business where they faced a quarrelsome partner in the person of the drinks mogul VJ Mallya, plus bits and bobs in Portugal and Finland. Carlsberg came to rue the day they signed the sales contract because in 2009 the Russian beer market started its decline.

Heady deals, no questions asked

In the Noughties, the global brewing industry was levelling out, but not everyone was equally equipped to make the most of this. In this respect, the ranking of the world's major brewers in 2000 makes interesting reading. Of the 30 leading brewers at the time, the majority have since disappeared, either because they were sold (fully or partially) or because they merged with each other. That may illustrate why the Noughties will go down as the decade of heady dealmaking and why the guys who could put together these pricey deals became the toast of town.

Not only did the total value of deals rise from hundreds of millions of dollars to billions, the multiples paid went through the ceiling, too. Whereas in the Nineties acquisitions were often valued at less than ten times EBITDA, double-digit multiples became very much the norm in the Noughties, rising as high as 19 times EBITDA. The most expensive deal of the Noughties – in terms of money spent – was InBev's takeover of Anheuser-Busch for USD $53 billion in cash in 2008. Still, the title for highest multiple ever paid probably has to go to Carlsberg, which bought the Chinese brewery Chongqing Brewery for 45 times earnings in 2010.[14] What were they thinking? Good question.

Leading Brewing Groups – 2000 (millions of hectolitres)

1	Anheuser-Busch	US	122.4	X
2	Heineken (excl. APB)	Netherlands	65.7	
3	AmBev	Brazil	59.7	X
4	Miller Brewing	US	49.0	X
5	SAB (excl. CR Snow, China)	UK	48.4	X
6	Interbrew (excl. Sun Interbrew, Russia)	Belgium	42.3	X
7	Grupo Modelo	Mexico	36.3	X
8	Asahi	Japan	29.7	
9	Coors	US	27.7	X
10	Kirin Group	Japan	27.1	
11	Carlsberg (excl. BBH)	Denmark	26.4	
12	FEMSA Cerveza	Mexico	23.3	X
13	Tsingtao	China	18.1	
14	BBH Group	Finland/ Sweden	16.8	X
15	Foster`s	Australia	16.6	X
16	Diageo	UK	15.7	
17	Bavaria	Colombia	14.7	X
18	Polar	Venezuela	14.5	
19	San Miguel	Philippines	13.1	X
20	Pabst	US	13.1	X
21	Scottish & Newcastle (excl. BBH)	UK	12.8	X
22	Bass	UK	12.4	X
23	Yanjing	China	12.2	
24	Quinsa / Quilmes	Argentina	11.9	X
25	Kaiser	Brazil	11.2	X
26	BBAG	Austria	11.1	X
27	Molson	Canada	11.1	X
28	China Resources Enterprises (CR Snow)	China	10.8	
29	Sun Interbrew	Russia	10.5	X
30	Lion Nathan	NZ/Australia	9.8	X

X = brewer sold (including partial stakes) or merged. Source: Canadean

The schoolmarm's grading

Some brewers on the industry's league table were more voracious and risk-loving than others. Best in class were Interbrew, AmBev, SAB and Heineken. Before setting up Carlsberg Breweries with Orkla, few would have believed that Danish brewer Carlsberg would rise to become one of the big four brewers. They would have been right to have been sceptical, because Carlsberg's ascent is plainly down to luck. Had Carlsberg not opportunistically benefitted from the merger with Norway's Orkla, which gave them access to the profitable market in Russia, they would have never taken over S&N.

European brewers have been heavily reliant on acquisitions to boost growth. It almost seemed that M&A (mergers and acquisitions) was like a drug. Since 2000, brewers have clinched about 800 deals, mostly in China, and the largest 50 deals were worth a combined $200 billion, acquired at an average multiple of 12 times EV (enterprise value)/EBITDA, although this multiple has been rising as available targets have become more scarce.[15]

However, the ones who clearly saw which way the industry was heading, and acted upon it were the adventurous Belgians (Interbrew), the hard-boiled Brazilians (AmBev) and the no-fuss South Africans (SAB). Compared to the other two, AmBev had it easy. In the 1990s, Brazil was already one of the biggest and most profitable beer markets. The billions of dollars they earned there helped fund their forays elsewhere into Latin America. But they clearly had set themselves the target to become the world's biggest brewer in 1991 when they made advances to Anheuser-Busch to combine forces.[16] The Brazilians were turned down by the brash and arrogant Yankees. Nonetheless, they patiently laid in wait, plotted on and 17 years later their erstwhile plan to take over Anheuser-Busch finally came to fruition.

Unlike AmBev, Interbrew and SAB had to clinch many more deals in the 1990s to reach their respective ranks on the brewers' league table in 2000. While for the Belgians the desire to move away from their home turf was obviously influenced by the opportunities they saw elsewhere, SAB was driven out of South Africa in the early 1990s by the not-too-unrealistic fear that once the apartheid regime had collapsed, their cash-rich company would be nationalised. Rather than risk becoming a sitting duck, they decided to embark on an internationalisation course which would reduce their dependence on their domestic market. It needs to be pointed out that, contrary to Interbrew, AmBev, Heineken and Carlsberg, the South Africans never enjoyed the backing of big and dedicated family shareholders who would have been willing to stick by them no matter what happened. That may help explain why SAB always strove to clinch deals with complex structures, which might prove too difficult for any hungry predator to disentangle: the share-swapping arrangement with Castel in Africa in 2001, the takeover of US brewer Miller in 2002, and Colombia's brewer Bavaria in 2005, which gave each of the previous owners a stake in SABMiller in return.

If truth be told, Heineken entered the globalisation race late and probably only out of rivalry with Interbrew.

Unlike Interbrew, they were already the world's most international brewer in 1990 through their beer export and 'build and brew' tactic. But as they focused their initial purchasing efforts on their European fiefdom, which would have strained their finances to the limits, Heineken was forced to watch the more recklessly leveraged Interbrew sail away to further shores, like Russia and Canada. Though a laggard, Heineken eventually embarked on a catch-up course and moved into Russia, then India, and later into Mexico. That each time they would overpay, as some critics maintain, because they came late to the table, is all forgiven and forgotten today. Once AB-InBev has consummated its marriage with SABMiller, Heineken will be the world's number two brewer, although trailing the enlarged AB-InBev by a wide margin.

Leading Brewing Groups - 2015

1	AB-InBev	Belgium	409.9
2	SABMiller	UK	191.3
3	Heineken	Netherlands	188.3
4	Carlsberg	Denmark	120.3
5	China Resources Breweries	China	117.4
6	Tsingtao	China	70.5
7	Molson Coors	US/Canada	58.1
8	Yanjing	China	48.3
9	Kirin Group	Japan	43.1
10	BGI/Castel Group	France	29.8
11	Petropolis	Brazil	23.0
12	Efes	Turkey	20.7

Source: Barth Report

The year 2015 will prove momentous for the brewing industry not only because it will be the last time SABMiller appears in the league table. It may also be the last time Danish brewer Carlsberg automatically slots in behind Heineken. In 2016, the race for the title 'global number three brewer' began in earnest, which might see Carlsberg being relegated. Vying for this prestigious trophy is China's CR Beer, formerly known as China Resources Breweries. CR Beer used to be SABMiller's joint venture partner and the producer of the world's biggest beer brand by volume, Snow, selling more than 100 million hl in 2015. Another contender could be Molson Coors, whose volumes sales will rise significantly once it consolidates SABMiller's share in the US joint venture MillerCoors. Perhaps Carlsberg will be demoted even further should the consolidation in the Chinese beer market finally take off. There are three Chinese brewers among the world's ten largest, whose sales at this stage are mostly domestic. When will they begin to see the light and engage in dealmaking themselves? Clubbing together with a local partner would be a start.

As we foresee a major league table reshuffling soon, we have included in the 2015 global brewers' ranking Brazil's brewer Petropolis, another attractive takeover target, and Turkey's Efes. Without lifting a finger the two might find themselves among the world's top ten brewers in no time. And finally, should you still need proof that dealmaking was and continues to be the most profitable way ahead in the brewing industry, consider this: in 2000, the world's number one brewer, Anheuser-Busch, was only four times bigger in volume sales than Kirin, ranked tenth. Come 2015 and AB-InBev was almost 14 times bigger than its tenth largest rival.

Missing the boat

It is idle to speculate why US brewer Anheuser-Busch so blatantly missed the boat called globalisation. They did not even try swimming after it. They just stood on the shore and watched it disappear over the horizon. It may have had something to do with the St Louis frame of mind. Having pulled off the feat of becoming the leading brewer in the US with a market share close to 50 percent without doing any deals whatsoever, they had become the victim of their own success. After all, the US was and is the world's most profitable beer market by far. Whichever deal they could clinch would pale in profitability next to their US business. They probably thought: "why spend our well-earned profits on foreign adventures with unknown outcomes and get horsewhipped by our investors in return?" Also, had they not been good boys and ticked all the right boxes when they bought into Mexico's Grupo Modelo in 1993? Had they not set up rewarding licensing agreements from Canada, to Italy, Ireland, Spain, France and Japan and acquired a stake in China's Tsingtao Brewery?

It was probably a mixture of lethargy and – assumed – invincibility that Anheuser-Busch became a pushover in the Noughties, especially after InBev snatched the title as number one global brewer from it in 2004. Suddenly it was held against Anheuser-Busch that they had not ventured into central and eastern Europe in the 1990s. Well, they did. Spurred on to solve the trademark dispute with the Czech Budweiser once and for all, they tried to buy Budweiser Budvar. Heavens know how they had got the idea into their minds that the post-communist Czech government could be bulldozed and that they would get Budweiser Budvar on the cheap? Instead, they lived up fully to the stereotype of the sly, carpet bagging Yankee, when they opened the USD $1 million St Louis Cultural Centre in Budweiser's home town of Ceske Budejovice in about 1993, started a baseball team, kitted out a café, and began offering English-language lessons. If this was the extent of their PR efforts to win over the government, it rightfully came to nothing. It also did not go down well with Czech officials that August Busch III, in discussions, put his feet on the table (as rumour has it) and would only offer USD $55 million for Budweiser Budvar (again, according to rumour), which was, together with Pilsner Urquell, the leading export brewery in communist times and considered one of the five companies on which Czech national pride hinged.

The Czechs' response to Anheuser-Busch's overtures was less than enthusiastic, especially when the UK's beer pressure group, CAMRA, came to Budvar's aid with a letter, insinuating that August III 'in malicious intent was seeking the effective decimation of the Czech brewery that has spent most of the 20th century proudly refusing to prostrate itself at the feet of the Great Satan of the planet's – the universe's – brewing industry.'[17] In the end, Mr Busch's attempts were thwarted, the cultural centre was shut down and Anheuser-Busch continued to meet the Czechs in court.[18] How would the story have ended for Anheuser-Busch if the Third had offered, say, $200 million or $300 million and bought Budweiser Budvar? Having failed, he had to return to St Louis and spend the next decade in anticipation of the inevitable.

To do justice to Anheuser-Busch, they were not the only ones to lose out because of inertia. The pussyfooting Mexicans, who controlled the brewer Modelo, blew their chances too. In 2000 they ranked 7th behind Interbrew and ahead of Carlsberg (11th). They would have had money and a brand, Corona Extra, that many coveted. In addition, they were in a market that was becoming increasingly profitable. So what held them back from entering the fray? One interpretation is that it was their conceit, coupled with ignorance about of the ways of the world, and their ill-starred alliance with another ditherer, Anheuser-Busch. Instead of quarrelling with Anheuser-Busch in the courts in the 1990s, they should have shown more sense and said: "Right, August, let's be reasonable and stop this. We ought to be doing something big!" They did not. In 2013 the Mexicans sold their remaining stake in Modelo to AB-InBev.

The internationalisation and the globalisation of the brewing industry have had winners, losers, also-rans, and several that would come under the heading of collateral damage. But hey, what times we have had! Reflecting on all those deals of the past two decades, the English novelist Charles Dickens (1812–1870) comes to mind when, talking about the 18th century, he wrote: 'It was the best of times, it was the worst of times, it was the age of wisdom, it was the age of foolishness, it was the epoch of belief, it was the epoch of incredulity, it was the season of Light, it was the season of Darkness, it was the spring of hope, it was the winter of despair, we had everything before us, we had nothing before us, we were all going direct to heaven, we were all going direct the other way.' No one could have put it better.

AB-INBEV: THE GREATEST ROLL-UP IN HISTORY

It's a funny world out there. Remember when InBev bought Anheuser-Busch, the brewer of Budweiser, in 2008 for USD $53 billion? Almost all the world took note since it was portrayed as the hostile takeover of an American icon. Seven years on, in 2015, the since renamed AB-InBev proposed to take over SABMiller for $100 billion plus, but the takeover received little or no attention outside the business pages. Although it is the ultimate deal that reeks of size for size's sake, AB-InBev's eventual world domination in beer will merely be a welcome side-effect, a stepping stone to even greater things. As we heard on Wall Street, AB-InBev's real reason for wanting to buy SABMiller was laughably absurd. They could not get Coca-Cola at this point and took the opportunity to bulk up in beer instead.

AB-InBev and Coke is a perplexing thought, isn't it? However, Ian Shackleton, a Nomura analyst, already said in early 2015: 'The numbers are enormous but feasible. You could create more value [!] out of Coke than almost any other fast-moving consumer goods company.'[1] Rest assured, even while AB-InBev has its hands full with bedding down SABMiller, its strategists are already planning their next move. Whether it will be Coca-Cola or Pepsi or any other player in the beverage industry is for the moment idle speculation.

AB-InBev's rise to number one brewer was envisioned by the teetotaller Jorge Paulo Lemann (born 1939), a self-made Brazilian billionaire of Swiss origins, over 20 years ago. Our view may suffer from 'hindsight bias', a term coined by the two Israeli psychologist-economists Daniel

Kahneman and Amos Tversky,[2] referring to the way in which a random sequence of events is given a compelling narrative by judging it from its outcome. Either way, the plain facts are that in 1989 Mr Lemann and his two partners, Marcel Telles (born 1950) and Carlos Alberto Sicupira (born 1948), took over the 18 million hl Brazilian brewer Brahma for $50 million. A decade on they teamed Brahma up with its rival Antarctica to become AmBev. In 2004, through orchestrating an alliance with Interbrew, the Belgian brewer of Stella Artois, they created InBev. Four years later, they paid $53 billion for Anheuser-Busch. If this deal wasn't vertiginous enough, in 2013 AB-InBev dished out $20 billion for full control of Mexico's Grupo Modelo. And in 2015 AB-InBev offered in excess of $100 billion for SABMiller. Though clinching only a few headline-making deals in 25 years, the Brazilians spectacularly became the biggest and best in the brewing industry. In other words, from a mouse they bred an elephant.

A note to readers here: If in the following chapters we use 'the Brazilians' synonymously with InBev and AB-InBev it is because we believe that, despite the globalisation rhetoric, the 'nationality' of a firm still matters, especially with regard to fundamental aspects such as where the strategy is hatched and whose long-term commitment is strongest. Seen from this perspective, AB-InBev is a Brazilian company and the fact that it is domiciled in Belgium is probably only a matter of the tax benefits this brings. The question remains: How did they get so big?

SABMiller's late CEO Graham Mackay once pointed out that the global consolidation of the beer industry was something of a curiosity. There were limited financial advantages in combining beer businesses which had no geographical overlap. Playing devil's advocate, Mr Mackay seemed to put his own deals into doubt. But lo and behold, no. In defiance of obvious synergies, these horizontal transactions nevertheless did the trick: AB-InBev's and SABMiller's buy-and-build tactics led to a huge rise in profits and made their investors incredibly wealthy.

Those self-same investors probably could not care less that these deals awarded AB-InBev the unflattering title of a 'roll-up' company. To the likes of us, a roll-up company is the business equivalent of a vacuum cleaner. Seemingly indiscriminately, it will suck up everything that lies in its path. *The Economist* attested roll-ups a near-clinical addiction to doing takeovers and called AB-InBev 'the greatest roll-up in history'.[3] Once the SABMiller deal goes through, it said, AB-InBev will have 'wheeled and dealed its way to being the world's 13th-most-valuable firm.'

A Belgian upstart

The story of AB-InBev only began after Belgium's Interbrew and Brazil's AmBev combined to InBev in 2004. Before, each polished their own résumé in dealmaking which, in the case of AmBev, was fairly short. Having established some bridgeheads in neighbouring Latin American countries, their major deal in the 1990s was a merger: the combination of Brazil's two biggest brewers, Brahma and Antarctica, to form AmBev. Their acquisitions strategies differed: While AmBev focused on the money side of deals, Interbrew chased volume gains. The Belgians may lay claim to the title of serial acquirer since they did far more deals in the 1990s. But they had little to show for themselves when AmBev came along. In actual fact their dealmaking in the early Noughties in the UK, when they tried to take over both Bass and Whitbread, was a near disaster. This was reflected in their share price. Between 2000, the year of their stock market listing, and 2004, Interbrew's shares lost about 30 percent of their value. For PR reasons, the transaction with AmBev was sold to the public in the guise of a friendly 'alliance',[4] although Interbrew technically took over AmBev,[5] but it was the Brazilians who would henceforth run the show.

As we argued in the previous chapter, to play Beer Monopoly, brewers first had to become the leaders in their domestic markets. For Interbrew the formative year was 1986, when two Belgian family brewers Artois and Piedboeuf threw in their lot with each other to set up Interbrew. The timing was spot on. Belgium was a small market with an annual production of 14 million hl beer, and Interbrew's beer exports were paltry when compared with Heineken's. Whether the de Spoelberch clan (Artois) and the Van Damme family (Piedboeuf) were spurred on by Heineken's international success or had done their maths and had seen that 1+1=3 could work, the establishing of Interbrew would not have been possible without political goodwill. In Belgium, where ties between business and the government are strong, the merger encountered no opposition and immediately enjoyed a market share of about 60 percent. Interbrew's stake in Belgium's beer profit pool would have been even higher after the families had appointed a former car industry executive as CEO; it was José Dedeurwaerder who radically rationalised operations, invested in state-of-the-art brewing technology and improved productivity. Alas, Mr Dedeurwaerder's ruthless approach to cost-cutting, which spelt closure for nine breweries in Belgium, three in France and two in the Netherlands, plus redundancies, was not met with approval. Politicians moaned and Belgium's notoriously belligerent unions called for a month-long strike at Interbrew. Confronted with a national PR crisis and needing a scapegoat, Interbrew's owners had to part company with Mr Dedeurwaerder in 1993. Despite his inglorious exit, Mr Dedeurwaerder's efficiency drive had been timely. When the Iron Curtain fell down, Interbrew was cashed up and at the ready to pursue a strategy of growth through acquisitions.

For most of the 1990s, Interbrew's advances into central and eastern Europe and China mirrored SABMiller's tactics. Instead of pushing their portfolio of Belgian brands like Stella Artois, Leffe and Hoegaarden, they strove to build local brands, having realised that in emerging markets local mainstream beers would provide the platform onto which they could later place their higher-priced international brands. Analysts begged to differ. In those days bankers were only familiar with the Heineken model for international growth. They took one look at Interbrew's bulging brand portfolio – 200 brands eventually – and decided it was a liability rather than an asset. Apart from quibbles with the money men, Interbrew's owners had other worries too. The early piecemeal purchases in Hungary, Croatia, Romania and Bulgaria had failed to catapult Interbrew forward. Interbrew's continuing status as a middling brewer on the global stage was suddenly seen as a threat to its competitiveness. Moreover, its core western European markets – UK, France, Netherlands, and Belgium – showed troubling signs of maturity, and beer consumption had begun to drop.

To the outside world, Interbrew's true blue-blood beerage – two barons, two counts and a viscount sat on its board[6] – were a picture of harmony and unity as if everybody acted in concert to join the top flight in world brewing. However, internally there were disputes over debt levels and dissent over strategy. Well aware that they had to get a foothold in the North American market, much like SAB in the 1980s when the South Africans secretly bought and sold the cultish Rolling Rock brewery in Pennsylvania,[7] they looked around for options. The surprise occasion arose in 1995. Hans Meerloo, Mr Dedeurwaerder's replacement as CEO, scored a victory. After only a month-long courtship, he launched a white knight takeover bid for Labatt, the Canadian brewer under siege from a corporate raider. The logic behind this trans-continental deal was a novelty. It was the first time a brewer had bought into a market not for volume's sake but for profits alone. And it turned out a beauty. It freed Interbrew from its dependence on Europe, allowed it to enter a safely regulated duopoly and gave it access to the vast North American profit pool. More than this, it propelled Interbrew's standing in the world's ranking up by 14 places to third. However, Mr Meerloo was not allowed to enjoy the fruits of his daring bid, although Labatt probably paid for itself within a few years after ancillary businesses were sold off and it became the profit machine that helped Interbrew pay for its next acquisitions.[8] Unhappy with the Labatt price tag, the Van Dammes and the de Spoelberchs reportedly blamed Mr Meerloo for having overspent. Interbrew, which had previously been debt-free,[9] suddenly had to tackle a debt pile of $2 billion. Mr Meerloo resigned in 1995.

It may have been because of internal frictions among the owners that Interbrew's executive suite for the next few years felt deserted. Dispensing with a CEO, Johnny Thijs in Europe and Hugo Powell in Canada became Chief Operating Officers who reported to Chairman Paul De Keersmaeker, a former Belgian government minister and proxy for the owners. At the time, few questioned this unusual situation as it corresponded with Interbrew's motto to become 'the world's local brewer'. The moniker was intended to convey, both externally and internally, Interbrew's commitment to producing local beers and giving country managers full autonomy in business affairs. The Canadians were certainly happy that the Belgians did not take over and allowed them to run things their way. If anything, the personnel traffic within Interbrew went east rather than west. Several Canadians were promoted to key positions at Interbrew, including Mr Powell, who finally became CEO in 1999.

But the laissez-faire culture began to alter when Interbrew went to the stock market in 2000. It floated about 20 percent of the company, raising about $3 billion. Pocketing other people's money seemed preferable to having to allow bankers into its bed, in the words of Mr de Keersmaeker. The listing came at a price. It put Interbrew's profits under the magnifying glasses of analysts. Whereas Interbrew's tactics of buying the number one or two brewer locally answered to the rules of Beer Monopoly, which helped it more than triple its net income in five years to $500 million in 2001, and double turnover to $6.8 billion, analysts complained that Interbrew had failed to squeeze optimum profits from its businesses and had neglected to seriously push a global brand.[10] Trying to butter up the analysts, Mr Powell seized the opportunity to buy big again when the UK brewers Bass and Whitbread came on the market. Together, they would have awarded Interbrew an immediate number one position in the UK and the top position in the import category thanks to its 'reassuringly expensive' Stella Artois. Interbrew also made their entry into Germany, where around the same time the international brand Beck's was put on the block as well as a host of other breweries (Diebels, Gilde, Spaten). However, in the UK Interbrew had reckoned without Stephen Byers, the UK's Secretary of State for Trade and Industry, who threw out the British transactions, and in Germany it had underestimated the cumbersome process of amassing a significant market share.

While the flustered Belgians thought they had done everything according to the rule book – going after international brands and market leaders – the analysts remained unimpressed. Interbrew's latest acquisitions were simply in the wrong places. The English and the German beer markets remained fragmented and in decline. Besides, selling the equivalent of millions of Olympic-sized swimming pools of beer had lost its allure in the world of finance. The profit metric was soon to rule supreme. In this respect Interbrew was a straggler because a paragon of efficiency or profitability it was not. As the nit-picking analysts never failed to point out, Interbrew's profit/EBITDA margin (19 percent) was smaller than that of AmBev (36 percent) and Anheuser-Busch (28 percent).[11] When Interbrew's share price went through the floor, the Belgian owners became extremely concerned and in 2002 Mr Powell resigned as CEO. He was replaced by the hapless John Brock, a former soft drinks executive, who was tasked with picking up the pieces of a botched globalisation strategy and boosting profitability.

The obvious unit to face pressure from shareholders to show profit growth was Labatt, who Interbrew largely relied on to keep the train chugging along. By 2003, Labatt contributed about a third to Interbrew's EBITDA, but improving the bottom line by marking up their beers was a risky undertaking. Canada's two major brewers, Labatt and Molson, had unhesitatingly raised prices. However, they had inadvertently created a booming business in discount beer for independents. Brands that had previously been star performers, like Labatt Blue, fell out of favour and the beer industry had to fight sluggish beer consumption. A string of Labatt presidents, all Canadians, fought these problems with limited success.[12] To do Interbrew's people justice, they overall increased profitability – Interbrew's profit margin climbed from a measly 13 percent in 1998 to 19 percent in 2003 – but their cost-cutting measures proved not to be radical enough.

Alliance with AmBev

At this stage, Interbrew would have benefitted greatly if their plan to buy SAB, codenamed 'Zulu', had come off. They could have sold investors the spin that both companies had pursued a similar strategy of seeking growth through deals in emerging and mature markets without much geographical overlap. It was not to be. SAB decided to move on and combine with Miller in the US, which certain conservative elements within Interbrew thought just as well, deeming the tie-up a deal too far.[13] This left Interbrew's Alexandre van Damme to pull off the stunning merger with AmBev in 2004. It created InBev, the world's largest brewer by volume – but not by profit, because that distinction still belonged to Anheuser-Busch.

The Belgian owners would have had their own reasons for allying themselves with the Brazilians, but they refrained from sharing them with the public. In a dilemma, Mr Brock resorted to reiterating brewers' standard excuse for sagging sales. At a meet-and-greet in the winter of 2004/2005 he told a hall full of incredulous Belgian officials that the alliance with AmBev would not only expand Interbrew's reach, it would insulate the group from the calamities of rainy summers in the northern hemisphere. Whatever the guests thought of this explanation, they kept it to themselves. The fact is, it soon emerged that the deal was very much to the Brazilians' advantage. Although the Brazilians would own a smaller stake in InBev than the Belgians, the two sides secretly agreed to stick together for 20 years and follow Mr Lemann's guiding light through thick (the deals to come) and thin (the risks). Publicly,

Interbrew and AmBev would operate independently in different hemispheres, maintain separate stock market listings, name four directors each to InBev's board, and keep Mr Brock as CEO – for the time being. His three-year contract was not renewed in 2005.

In view of those structural complexities it took observers a while to figure out AmBev's ultimate goal. Having purchased a significant stake in Argentina's brewer Quilmes in 2002, AmBev had become the major brewer in South America. What AmBev was really after was full control of the Americas, the most prized 'streets' in Beer Monopoly. Labatt would provide a missing piece: a stake in the Canadian and the Mexican markets (through its 30 percent shareholdings in FEMSA). True, the US didn't yet feature and Mexico would soon be out of the picture when FEMSA unwound its relationship with Labatt a few months later. AmBev had clearly foreseen this possibility. In a US filing AmBev had put a valuation to Labatt without the FEMSA stake. The loss of FEMSA notwithstanding, the Brazilians kept their cool because they already knew this trifling matter would be taken care of a few years later. When InBev bought Anheuser-Busch it also obtained half of Mexico's other brewer, Grupo Modelo, which boasted an even more attractive international brand, Corona Extra.

Labatt became the key negotiating chip. Interbrew effectively sold Canada to AmBev in exchange for a controlling stake in the Brazilian company, thus fulfilling AmBev's ambition to become the number two player in the Americas in terms of EBITDA ($1.6 billion), or the number three in the world behind Anheuser-Busch ($4.1 billion) and Heineken ($1.9 billion), when excluding Interbrew's remaining profits ($1.5 billion).

If media were baffled by the deal's intricacies, so were investors. Shares of each company went on a tumultuous ride. Several commentators argued that AmBev had walked away with Interbrew's tastiest morsels and left itself an escape route in case the alliance floundered. Nothing could have been further from AmBev's intention. Had journalists managed to quiz Mr Lemann he might have told them, referring to TV entertainment's most quotable character, Blackadder's Lord Flashheart: "I've got a plan, and it's as hot as my pants!"

Unbeknownst to us, his bold and doggedly pursued ambition had been to build the 'Coca-Cola of beer', a brewing company to dominate the world, by taking over stable focused businesses with high margins and market shares. When he approached Anheuser-Busch's CEO August Busch III in the mid-1990s to help him realise it, Mr Busch failed to see its upside.[14] The Belgians did.

Running things the Brazilian way

Being exceedingly media-shy, statements from Mr Lemann are rare. On buying Brahma in 1989, he reportedly said that all around Latin America the richest guys had been brewers. However, the rest of the statement, usually dropped, is even more pertinent. "These guys couldn't all be geniuses. It's the business that must be good."[15] The beer business could be very good – read profitable – indeed, provided brewers took to heart Mr Lemann's maxims. On a list, handed out to his employees at Garantia, an investment firm, which he took over in 1971, one read: 'Innovations that create value are useful, but copying what works well is more practical.'[16]

As a matter of fact Mr Lemann's business credo is an amalgam of other peoples' doctrines. Allegedly, Messrs Lemann, Telles and Sicupira learnt from Sam Walton, the founder of US retailer Walmart, to bludgeon suppliers to deliver low prices; they are said to have picked up from the Japanese the principles of lean manufacturing, benchmarking and efficiency programmes; and adopted from Jack Welch, the decades-long CEO of General Electric, the '20-70-10' rule, which says: promote the top 20 percent of your employees, maintain the 70 in the middle and fire the rest.

Unquestionably, these principles would have made the Brazilians very demanding employers and hot on the scent for cost savings. The aphorism 'Costs are like fingernails. You have to cut them constantly.' is attributed to Mr Sicupira. Stories are legion of how the Brazilians, once they took control of a company, rationed pens and paper, cut off electricity for elevators, took mobile phones away and made sales people pay for a company car wash out of their own pockets. Again and again, we were told by former employees, still under the effects of shell shock, how they tore down walls, got rid of personal desks and even offices altogether. The most radical solution was probably found in balmy Brazil. Several years ago a group of perhaps 80 of AmBev's sales people were seen having an al fresco meeting outside AmBev's building in Sao Paulo, sitting under some kind of marquee which had been kitted out with benches and tables for this purpose.

The Brazilians' gloves-off style shook up the staid world of brewers, with staff and suppliers – the notorious 'Dutch Auctions' – being the first to feel the Brazilians' fervour. Employees' horror stories, which kept the brewers' grapevine abuzz during the Noughties, made industry veterans tap their noses. We in the northern hemisphere had seen nothing yet, they said. The AmBev guys not only refused to live up to our cliché of Brazil as a carefree country of beaches and bikinis; their enforcers, who soon appeared all over the Interbrew empire, were but vanguards of a revolution about to happen.

Labatt was the first to get a taste of things to come. Before succeeding Mr Brock as CEO of InBev, the Brazilian Carlos Brito (born 1960), an engineer who had joined Brahma in the early 1990s to head sales and then operations, becoming AmBev's CEO in 2003, made a name for himself in Canada. In 2004 he was sent north to knock Labatt into shape. Within months of his arrival Mr Brito shut two breweries and fired 20 percent of Labatt's salaried workforce. Not wasting time, Mr Brito set out to implement a plan that had been honed and fine-tuned in Brazil over a decade ago, his 'Brazilian blueprint' for running a lean and mean beer profit machine.

Having previously only dealt with emerging markets, where beer consumption was on the rise, Labatt became the first company where Mr Brito and his people could demonstrate to investors that the Brazilians were capable of running a business in a mature market more efficiently than the previous lot. Labatt was turned into their test laboratory for proving 1+1=3.

Learning from the best

It is one thing to copy and paste others' how-to manuals; it is another to put them into practice and do so successfully. This is what the quartet of Lemann, Telles, Sicupira and Brito did, first at Brahma, then at AmBev. According to the economist Donald Norman Sull, who has succinctly analysed Brahma's rise,[17] when Mr Lemann and his partners bought Brazil's major brewer in 1989 and made Mr Telles CEO, without anybody having a background in brewing or knowing much about the industry, they saw that Brahma's smaller rival Antarctica was one step ahead in terms of profitability and new product launches. They set out to change this. Their initial hypothesis was: if we could start from scratch, which type of brewery would we build, and where? They visited several friendly brewers around the world for ideas. Home again, they drew up a plan of their ideal factory and where best to roll it out over Brazil, having realised that Brahma had far too many, most of which were too small, operated inefficiently and churned out beer of inconsistent quality. Not shying away from extreme solutions, between 1989 and 1991 they closed more than ten plants. In 1996 they built their first state-of-the-art brewery in Rio with a capacity of 12 million hl. Capital investment into modernising and rebuilding plants came to over $2.5 billion in the 1990s.

As operational improvements only go so far in raising efficiencies, they next strove to reduce headcount. From 1990 to 1998 Brahma cut the labour force by half to 10,700, in order to achieve world class productivity, which is measured in volumes produced per employee.

The same approach was taken to distribution. Having studied Anheuser-Busch's relations with its distributors, Brahma introduced a system of incentives and metrics for its distributors. Since distribution is a volume business, where bulk is shifted for little profit, they nudged out the underperforming distributors, and cut their number from 1,000 in 1989 to 300 in 1999, while increasing their average size and distributors' profits.

All these steps may have been introduced with an eye to their competitor Antarctica. But their obsession with cost reduction was triggered by a formative event: the introduction of the Real as Brazil's currency in 1994 which ended years of hyperinflation. Under hyperinflation it had been easy to pass cost inefficiencies on to the consumers via price increases. That changed with the Real. Disposable income rose and with it the demand for beer, but consumers became price-conscious too. Brahma responded quickly by setting itself aggressive cost reduction targets, which were meant to serve as an insurance for hard times.[18]

There were quite a few. A threat to their business had risen in the Kaiser beer brand. Launched in 1982 by local Coca-Cola bottlers as a low-price beer, Kaiser had gained market share quickly and eaten into the sales of Brahma's flagship brand. Mr Telles responded by making the growth of Skol, the company's second brand, a priority. It helped that Mr Telles had kept the Brahma and Skol distributors separate. Priced below Brahma and bolstered by product and packaging innovations plus a marketing campaign, keen and eager distributors made

Skol the fastest growing beer in Brazil between 1994 and 2000. Another menace to their business would have been the loss of the Pepsi licence in 1994, a multi-million hl business, although Brahma pretended that they had not renewed the ten-year agreement in order to focus more fully on their own soft drink brands. However, after Pepsi's subsequent licence holder, Baesa, went bankrupt and Pepsi sweetened the deal by throwing in several modern factories plus infrastructure to prevent another bottler from going under, Brahma in 1997 agreed to re-establish their relationship, this time for 20 years. In 2015 AmBev was the largest Pepsi bottler outside the US.

You step on the bus or you're not on the bus

It was in those years that Brahma's approach to doing business became identical with meticulous attention to detail, cost cutting, efficiency drives, profit growth and scant regard for people. Under their regime jobs had been axed by the thousands. However, if truth be told, Brahma's turnaround to a world-class beer business would not have been possible without a dedicated staff. You simply cannot run a company with chieftains alone. It was pointed out that Brahma has always striven to recruit the brightest and best young people, who fitted their profile, known by its acronym: PSD, for 'poor, smart, deep desire to get rich.'[19] To match their devotion and enthusiasm the Brazilians devised a meritocratic compensation system. 'Considerable rewards, in cash and equity, are available to those who hit tough targets at company, unit and individual level. Miss them and bonuses vanish.'[20]

Some have decried the Brazilians' claim that 'people are at the centre' as deeply cynical. What critics fail to see is that the Brazilians adhere to a different view of human nature. Whereas in post-materialist societies the notion of 'homo reciprocans' – the bearded tree-hugger who altruistically wants to make the world a better place – prevails, the Brazilians favour 'homo oeconomicus', a tough cookie, who is exclusively motivated by self-interest. Their reliance on clear metrics to steer and measure staff performance not only matches this view, it also functions as a safeguard against key knowledge leaving the company through the revolving doors. As we see it, their reducing of work/labour to a set of metrics was merely another component of their ultimate scheme to design an all-encompassing numbers-based model for running the best beer company. This model was not just applied to Brazil. It would have been Mr Lemann's intention to develop a genuine one-fits-all blueprint, whose fundamentals could be put to work anywhere. Once they felt confident of that, Mr Lemann decided that Brahma should start playing Beer Monopoly.

Merging Brahma and Antarctica

But first they had to do their homework and consolidate the Brazilian market. They had to take over their smaller rival Antarctica. The chance presented itself in 1999. Antarctica faced a serious liquidity crisis, which was partly triggered by recent beer price wars to fend off upstarts like Kaiser and Schincariol and their cheaper beers. Almost suicidally, Antarctica had instigated many of the most bruising price reductions, which meant a serious depletion of its profits.

Add to that Antarctica's high gearing at the time the Real was devalued in 1999 and the company had to fear going belly up when presented with the interest bill for its dollar-denominated debt. Brahma, on the other hand, enjoyed a financial cushion, thanks to its rabid cost reductions. And so Brahma came along waving wads of money.[21]

Brahma would not have been the only brewer interested in acquiring Antarctica. Anheuser-Busch held a small stake in Antarctica. Ironically, the Americans misjudged the situation, thinking that the Brazilian regulator would never wave a deal through that would combine the country's number one and two brewers and give the resulting entity a market share of about 70 percent. They were wrong. Brazil has long been a protectionist economy. Fearing that Anheuser-Busch would take advantage of the crisis and scoop up a Brazilian company cheaply in the manner of other foreign multinational companies, the government allowed Brahma and Antarctica to merge. It would have helped that Mr Lemann had deployed a team of advisors to the antitrust agency, who presented the tie-up as a matter of economic sovereignty, which would create a national champion too large to be taken over by a foreign brewing giant.[22] This left Anheuser-Busch with two options: join the Brazilians' table as a junior partner and help establish a beer behemoth in the Americas, or back out completely and sell their stake in Antarctica to the newly formed AmBev. Fatally, they took the easy way out.

Had Mr Busch III known that Mr Lemann had already used some cash from the sale of his Garantia investment house in 1997 to buy a stake in the shaving firm Gillette, and won a seat on its board, he might have decided differently. As the journalist Alex Cuadro tells it, Mr Lemann only invested in Gillette to spend time with the veteran American investor and 'sage of Omaha', Warren Buffett, another Gillette board member. 'In board meetings, he impressed Buffet with his quiet, thoughtful style, and they became friends.'[23] This friendship would have dire consequences for Anheuser-Busch. After Mr Lemann had persuaded Mr Buffett to part with his shares in the US brewer (Mr Buffett was the second biggest shareholder with a 4.9 percent stake), he knew that other investors would follow and Anheuser-Busch would be a done deal.

Once InBev was formed, Anheuser-Busch became a sitting target. It would have been in 2005 that analysts openly began to discuss InBev taking over the US brewer. Gagged by their contract, the self-same 'conservative elements' within InBev's Belgian owners, who had opposed a deal with SAB, now fell in line behind Mr Lemann's strategy. Stopping the CEO carousel was the first outward sign that boardroom discords were a thing of the past. Mr Brito was installed as CEO at the end of 2005 and has run the company ever since. So overwhelming must have been the owners' support for Mr Brito that he was allowed to phase out the Belgian managers from executive positions and replace them with Brazilians. The Brazilian imports were not only more familiar with Mr Brito's blueprint for running a beer profit machine, they also had no qualms in setting it to work quickly even if it meant ruffling quite a few feathers. Belgium, the new group's headquarters, was not spared. Regardless of protests and strikes, the headcount was reduced to 3,000 from 9,000 and breweries were shut down as the Brazilians transformed InBev into a finance-led company. Ironically or not, in August 2016 the socialist mayor of Leuven, where the company is headquartered, recommended Mr Brito be made a citizen of honour.

Becoming finance-led amounted to no less than a full-scale makeover; InBev's game became all about money. The company's annual report for 2005 clearly stated it for all to see. Dropping all reference to beer, it read: 'Our financial results show that we are on track to achieve our vision – going from Biggest to Best. There are many ways, of course, for a company to measure "best". In terms of profitability, reaching our goal of a 30 percent EBITDA margin by the end of 2007 is a simple and straightforward way of tracking it.'

Beer became of secondary importance, a means to an end, which spelt 'profit rise'. We dare say had the Brazilians seen the chance of achieving a similarly spectacular profit boost through dealmaking by peddling soap or washing powder, they might have done it. But beer just happened to be a better business.

Speaking finance fluently

Ultimately, when Mr Brito applied his hack-'n'-slash scheme to InBev, much more was at stake than making the Interbrew-AmBev alliance work. InBev had to start speaking a language that investors would understand. To this end, they had to prove they could grow profits in both emerging and mature markets. In the emerging market of Brazil this had been easy. Enjoying a market share of around 70 percent and controlling distribution, size alone became a big advantage, which made profits bubble ever more vigorously. In mature markets, with true competition and no consumption growth, raising profits was much harder. But the same merciless approach to costs that worked in Brazil also led to higher profits in western Europe. Within two years of taking over, the Brazilians saved InBev about $300 million a year through plant closures, layoffs, shared procurement and services, and the like.[24]

Choosing money over beer, bankers and investors became InBev's addressees. The Brazilians left it to their brands to speak to the consumers. Again, in an effort to reduce complexities and prevent confusion, they decided to kill off Interbrew's strategy of being the 'world's local brewer'. Out of nearly 300 brands, they began 'prioritising a small group with greater growth potential within each relevant consumer segment', as they said in their 2005 annual report. That year the brand line-up included Stella Artois, Brahma, Beck's and Leffe. In 2008, it included Budweiser, Stella Artois and Beck's. In 2015 it was Budweiser, Corona Extra and Stella Artois. These changes are far from accidental. They underline that for the Brazilians old habits and tradition ('we have always done it this way') do not count. As we argue in the Introduction: what's past is past, or, in business parlance: 'a merchant does not spend any money on what-has-been.'

It was through planning the future that the Brazilians sought to secure profit growth. In a way, investors are like trophy wives. They do not love you for the presents you lavished on them in the past. They always want more. Understanding this psychology, the Brazilians knew they had to hold out to their investors the prospect of a Porsche this year and a Ferrari next – and stick to their promise. In this respect, planning became the prerequisite for creating shareholder value. Coined by Jack Welch in the 1980s, the term has since fallen into disrepute. Nevertheless, the principle still dominates the corporate world. Only if management can grow sales, profits and cash flow over time will share prices rise.

While keeping shareholders sweet was important, planning coupled with reliability would become the Brazilians' most valuable currency in gaining bankers' trust. First, they needed to align their planning with the financial industry's. After all, what do bankers and investors want? First, they want to see a plan that shows how a creditor intends to pay down his debt; finance capital is impatient and seeks short-term gains. Second, the Brazilians needed to demonstrate reliability. Banks live off fees from deals and interest from debt. If a creditor presents them with a plan as to how he will pay them back, they make his plan theirs. Once a debtor has hit his self-set targets 100 percent – not 103 percent, not 95 percent – several times over, his reliability is converted into trust.

Bankers are not interested in how creditors reach those targets. They literally do not care if Mr Brito follows a premiumisation strategy by selling a commodity at a higher price, or cuts costs by one dollar per hl. They only seek evidence that he lives up to his forecasts and adheres to financial indicators that are meaningful to bankers, for example EBITDA, Return on Investment, dividends, EBIT margin, interest cover, debt levels. Those key financial indicators (KPIs) will be listed in the loan agreements. Not all of them stand up to pure reason. Why, for example, is a debt level of two times EBITDA acceptable to bankers, but a level beyond or above is not? In the case of the former, bankers will ask "Why don't you do anything with your money?" In the case of the latter, they will worry "How will you pay down your debt?"

Because of the arbitrariness of some financial KPIs, common-sense objections to planning are manifold. It is called glorified guesswork, a fantasy, about as realistic in its outcome as reading tea leaves. Indeed, once upon a time we were the playthings of fate and the future was unknowable. However, in the 1990s, thanks to trillion-fold increases in computing power, companies and bankers developed ways and means – planning models – in which the future could be measured and assessed in terms of probabilities. Planning became the tool to eliminate unpredictability, turning chance and risk into something that could be handled, or so it was thought.

Company valuations were among the first to benefit from the assumed eradication of risk. Previously breweries had been bought and sold on the basis of their net asset value, typically their bricks and mortar minus liabilities. Valuations were a snapshot of the present. By the mid-1990s companies were increasingly sold on hopes for the future, or whatever you like to call projected future earnings given in EBITDA multiples. In essence, the multiple is the number of years a buyer would have to own an acquired firm, while maintaining its current profits before his purchase outlay was paid back. Naturally, no one assumes profits to stay flat. Buoyed by the unquestioned view that future profitability would be better than past profitability, prices for brewing companies duly went through the roof.

King of planning

In the brewing industry, AB-InBev became the undisputed supremo of planning. Its fiendishly complex system, based on what is called Zero-Based Budgeting (ZBB), took root in InBev's culture in 2006. McKinsey calls ZBB 'a repeatable process that organisations use to rigorously review every dollar in the annual budget, manage financial performance on a monthly basis, and build a culture of cost management among all employees.'[25] The Brazilians did not limit it to one cost aspect, like personnel, as is commonly held against them, but employed ZBB to develop deep visibility into all cost drivers and then used that visibility to set credible budget targets. This meant that cutting costs was not self-serving. In the UK, the Brazilians allegedly saved $325,000 by telling employees to use double-sided black-and-white printing, which they then spent on hiring more sales people. If applied correctly, ZBB allows you to surgically cut the fat and help build up organisational muscle.[26]

Aiming for the – non-ironic – accolade of 'a cheapskate, a tight-fist and a penny-pinching git', a praise for the most efficient company coined by craft brewer BrewDog, the Brazilians came to know every aspect of their business like the back of their hand and helped them save cash. Both would stand them in good stead. In the Noughties cash was king, so much so that InBev began hoarding it, for example by deferring payments to its suppliers. Stretching the gap between when companies got paid by their customers and when they paid their suppliers became so fashionable that the once-onerous debt to the supplier was reinvented as 'interest-free credit'.

What some thought of as objectionable payment terms were merely a sign of the new times. In the Noughties debt became a good thing, basically indispensable if, in dealmaking, a company could use other people's money to increase its profits many times over.

Critics have accused the Brazilians of not being brewers but bankers, but that was the whole point of the exercise. In the past three decades, finance has been the proverbial tail that wags the dog. Knowing full well that the brewing industry's fetishistic obsession with beer volume growth was outdated, the Brazilians and the South Africans at SAB were the first to grasp that there is a dichotomy between business and industry, and that they had to cross over to the other side to secure finance capital. The difference between industry and business is that industry makes or does something and money is a side-product; the purpose of a business is simply to make money. As the financial industry views everything as a business, the two brewers embraced its principles ahead of their rivals, whether they kept up appearances as a brewer (SABMiller) or dropped the pretence altogether (AB-InBev).

It was through obsessively detailed planning and the predictable hitting of targets again and again that the Brazilians gained a reputation as reliable debtors. They therefore had no trouble going after Anheuser-Busch at the height of the 2008 financial crisis which threatened to devastate the global economy. By that stage InBev had become Too Big To Fail (no irony intended). When they passed their hat around, the bankers threw money at them, secure in the belief that the Brazilians would pay it back, come hell or high water.

By 2008, and certainly after the Anheuser-Busch takeover, the Brazilians would have cemented their company's standing as a dependable and reliable roll-up in the world of finance that knew how to deliver. 'Delivering' in their case meant the consistent, dramatic upsurges in profitability after each deal. Hiking EBITDA in AmBev, then in InBev, and next in AB-InBev, was taken as evidence of a repeatable model at work.[27]

Roll-ups, in our view, do not just have an innate desire to grow bigger through takeovers. Sometimes, their dealmaking has a defensive element too. It may help disguise the fact that under current circumstances a company's options for simple revenue growth are finite. This would have been obvious to the analysts who pointed out before the Anheuser-Busch takeover that InBev had no culture of top-line growth. By this they meant that in many markets InBev had failed to show that they could increase their turnover by selling more beer and pushing up market shares. Again, Labatt is a good example. Under the Brazilians' regime, Labatt's profit rise between 2004 and 2007 was certainly dazzling, but so was the decline in turnover. Fortunately, just when investors might have started asking pointed questions, InBev bought Anheuser-

Busch and this embarrassing detail was hidden from view. AB-InBev's 2009 turnover in North America (US and Canada combined) jumped to $15.5 billion thanks to the full consolidation of Anheuser-Busch's turnover. It rose slightly to $16.0 in 2012, after which it stayed flat until 2014. In 2015 it declined to $15.5 billion. Then again, did investors care? Obviously not. Cleverly, the Brazilians had chosen instead to highlight a set of figures which was much more to investors' liking: EBITDA. Not only was it sizeable by industry standards; between 2000 and 2010 the Brazilians also scored double-digit profit growth annually, the most worshipped idol in the financial sector

The takeover of Anheuser-Busch

Armed with an impressive track record in dealmaking that was proving that the total worth of a joint enterprise was greater than the sum of its individual parts, the Brazilians went after Anheuser-Busch in June 2008 to create the world's number one brewer and retake the crown from SABMiller. Cautious to call the deal a 'combination', the Brazilians launched an audacious all-cash offer, which valued Anheuser-Busch in excess of $40 billion. The takeover attack made headline news all around the world, not least because the battle immediately became nasty. August Busch IV, who had by then succeeded his father as CEO, rejected the offer. His team appealed to patriotic, if not old-fashioned jingoistic, sentiments in their defence, prompting a hostile InBev to bluster about removing the brewer's board. Anheuser-Busch wound up suing, accusing InBev of lying in its communications to shareholders.

Viewed as American an icon as apple pie, Anheuser-Busch had been led by members of the Anheuser or Busch families for most of its past 156 years. But the Buschs owned less than 5 percent of the shares in aggregate and had no power to block the takeover.

A month later the pandemonium was over, after InBev had raised its bid to $70 per share from $65, a massive premium over the level at which Anheuser shares had traded ($52) before any talk of a deal had arisen. The final offer valued Anheuser-Busch at $53 billion, which meant AB-InBev had to take on about $45 billion in debt, an amount it was able to cull from ten different banks around the world. Its debt level shot to 4.7 times profits (EBITDA) at the end of 2008. Surely motivated by a bonus scheme totalling $1.3 billion, which was to be shared by Mr Brito and a crew of 40 executives, they dramatically lowered the debt level to 1.9 times EBITDA, below the critical level, by the end of 2012.

In terms of dollars alone the deal would have appeared expensive, although in profit multiples (12.4 times EBITDA) it probably matched what Interbrew had paid for Labatt. However, this time around only one person voiced his reservations. In the heat of the takeover battle SABMiller's CEO Graham Mackay opined that it would be very difficult for InBev to obtain savings which justified the offered price as Anheuser-Busch was known to be one of the most competitive – read leanest – brewers in the world. He would say that, wouldn't he, as the Brazilians were about to invade his turf. Ever the smooth-talking low-hitter, Mr Mackay had chosen his words carefully. He said: "One wonders how InBev intends to reach such high savings, without damaging the business in the process."[28] Investors thought differently. They were confident that within four years AB-InBev would have recouped their investment – and they were right.

Once the deal was done, the Brazilians immediately whipped out their blueprint, which had served them well before, and buckled down. Like they had done at Labatt and at InBev, the new foreign owners swung the axe at the acquired firm. Within months 14 of Anheuser-Busch's 17 top executives had left. In no time they cut about 3,000 jobs, revamped the compensation system and abolished perks that had made Anheuser-Busch's employees the envy of others. Observers rubbed their eyes when they saw how many low-hanging fruit the Brazilians could pick. Contrary to Mr Mackay's judgment, it turned out the American brewer had not been run very competitively or efficiently.

Never slow to take action, the Brazilians also cleared out Anheuser-Busch's attic quickly. By the end of 2009 they had already passed their goal of selling off $7 billion in assets, divesting aluminium can plants in the US as well as breweries in Europe and South Korea and a stake in Chinese brewer Tsingtao. Gone too was Busch Entertainment, which controlled the SeaWorld and Busch Gardens theme parks. The disposals followed two rationales. The first straightforward objective would have been to reduce the debt level. The second one would have been to set Anheuser-Busch free from its non-beer entanglements. Generally speaking, analysts do not like conglomerates. A group's profit margins suffer if it is spread over various not-so-profitable industries. Besides, conglomerates make comparisons difficult for analysts. Additionally, there is a higher risk for a deal to trip up and not deliver the assumed gains if there are too many units that might end up in trouble of their own.

However, the disposals of breweries in Europe and China followed another logic easily understood in the financial industry. Reading like a commandment it says: 'You do not burden yourself with investments that you cannot grow in value. They are like dead capital.' In China, both InBev and Anheuser-Busch had their separate businesses, which in the case of Anheuser-Busch included a 27 percent stake in Tsingtao. Reviewing the Anheuser-Busch-InBev deal, which would have raised their combined market share in China to 15 percent, the Chinese regulator decided to bar AB-InBev from hiking their stake in Tsingtao. As a 27 percent stake was too small to give them a big say, the Brazilians went for an exit, flogging off a chunk to Japan's brewer Asahi and the rest to a Chinese tycoon, while pocketing $900 million. The Brazilians would not regret the sale. In 2015 AB-InBev's market share in China was 15 percent, up from 8 percent in 2007.

It might have pained the Belgians that the Brazilians chose to dump InBev's breweries in central and southeast Europe, which the old Interbrew had arduously built up through acquisition, but Europe has never held the Brazilians' interest. Its mature markets are simply past their prime and will never produce significant profit growth. Hence the unit was sold to the private equity firm CVC, which has since handed it on to brewer Molson Coors. The sale of South Korea's Oriental Brewery to a group of private equity outfits would have appeared to follow the same course, until it was revealed that the Brazilians had only exchanged it for cash so that the temporary owners could milk Oriental before AB-InBev bought the business back.

The missing piece

Our elaborate explanations notwithstanding, the Brazilians' whirlwind actions at Anheuser-Busch only had one aim: keeping bankers' trust. After all, they already had their next job lined up for them, which was to buy out Mexico's Grupo Modelo, the number one brewer in that country with a market share of more than 50 percent in a virtual duopoly with Heineken's FEMSA. In effect, Mexico was the last missing piece in the Brazilians' ambition to control the Americas, the most valuable set of 'streets' in Beer Monopoly.

On the face of it, by taking over Grupo Modelo the Brazilians were only tying up loose ends. The old Anheuser-Busch had shared a bond with the Mexicans since 1993, when the Americans first took a stake in Grupo Modelo. They eventually built up a 50.4 percent economic stake, for which they paid a total of $1.6 billion, but the Mexican families had kept the majority of votes. In reality, the Brazilian roll-up wizards needed another profit injection. In Canada and the US they were about to lose their Midas touch as sales had started to go south. Most worryingly, in the all-important US, AB-InBev's market share had dropped to 45 percent in 2012 from the 49 percent when they bought Anheuser-Busch. Although they had succeeded in hiking the average price of beer and pushing up profits according to plan, this tactic would have its limitations.

By contrast, Mexico's beer market, the world's fourth most profitable, was growing at about 3 percent annually and yet Grupo Modelo was widely considered not to be a best-in-class business. The Mexican brewer had an EBITDA margin of only 30 percent whereas its peers in Latin America enjoyed a 50 percent margin. To the Brazilians all these aspects combined meant a huge opportunity awaited.

However, relations between AB-InBev and Grupo Modelo were fraught. After the sale of Anheuser-Busch the Mexicans launched arbitration proceedings, alleging they should have been consulted over any change in control of the stake. In 2010, the arbitration panel ruled in favour of AB-InBev. Once the bold Brazilians had joined Grupo Modelo's board, some family members would have put pressure on the others to sell, probably arguing that big bucks were better than dividends.

It would have also dawned upon the Mexicans that they had not played Beer Monopoly to their full advantage. They owned an aspirational brand, Corona Extra, alright. Did they do anything with it? Hardly, as they had remained stuck in the internationalisation mindset. Relying on beer exports, 85 percent of which went to the US and Canada, they had failed to embark on a global buy-and-build mission. Above all, time was not on their side. The Brazilians were the only buyer around. Who could say whether their offer would remain on the table indefinitely?

Ignorant of these various machinations, outsiders would have thought that the Brazilians were following some sort of Olympic four-year cycle when they announced in 2012 that they had clinched an agreement to buy the rest of Grupo Modelo for $20 billion. This seemed like an excessively steep price considering that the whole of Grupo Modelo had a market value of $23 billion before word of the deal came out. This would not have deterred the Brazilians, who always seemed disposed to splash out if they wanted a company badly. Mr Brito's justification confirms this. "We feel very good about the price we paid," he said. "We paid a premium for 50 percent of the company but we got 100 percent of the synergies and a business that was not ours before."[29]

To finance the all-cash transaction AB-InBev said it had added $14 billion of new bank loans, adding that it would reduce its net debt to 2.0 times EBITDA during 2014.

However, there was a hurdle. In the US, Grupo Modelo operated through an importer, Crown Imports, which the Mexicans jointly owned with the US drinks group Constellation Brands. Trying to appease the US anti-trust watchdogs, the Brazilians offered to sell Grupo Modelo's stake to Constellation Brands. If AB-InBev had bought out Constellation Brands and distributed the beer itself, it would have pushed its market share in the US above 50 percent, which would have made the regulators see red. Instead, by making Constellation Brands their exclusive US partner, the Brazilians would step back while actually remaining in charge.

Spoiling their game

To the Brazilians' surprise, the US regulators threw out the plan. Not being fools, the regulators saw that the arrangement would boost AB-InBev's pricing power no end. Being the number one brewer in the US, AB-InBev had already used its muscle to hike prices overall, as MillerCoors, the number two, could likewise be trusted to do – albeit after a bit of a time lapse to defy accusations of collusion. Constantly raising prices for their beers may have run counter to classical economics which assumes that competing beer producers would pursue market share expansion by lowering prices. But what did classical economics know about finance and its dictates of profit growth? The only market participant to spoil AB-InBev's and MillerCoors' sport was Crown Imports, the importer of Corona Extra, with a 7 percent market share. A rogue player to the core, it did not follow their example, although, as the major import brand, Corona Extra was considered to have a higher value and price. By not increasing prices in sync with the big brewers, and thus narrowing the gap in retail prices from above, Corona Extra had succeeded in taking sales away from AB-InBev.

It did not take the regulators long to figure out the real reason why AB-InBev wanted to buy Grupo Modelo: they were not after Corona Extra's market share; they were only interested in indirectly utilising Crown Imports to move prices up across all segments. Imagine the possibilities: had AB-InBev jacked up prices by, say, 3 percent, it would earn around $1 billion more in profit every year.[30] This was not to be. In 2013, the regulators forced AB-InBev to sell one of their breweries in Mexico to Constellation Brands plus the perpetual rights for the Corona and Modelo brands in the US for about $2.9 billion.

Had the Brazilians been prone to fits of temper they might have thumped the table and shouted an expletive, but we would guess that feeling sorry for themselves is not a sentiment they would wallow in. Workaholics that they are, they would have flipped open their laptops and devised a plan as how to go about cracking their next takeover target. In the meantime their soldiers would have been given marching orders to streamline the Modelo business in the tried and tested fashion.

For a year, it seemed that all was going to plan at AB-InBev. Then black clouds began looming on the horizon. For one, there were troubling signs that global beer production had hit its peak in 2013. It declined in 2014, the first time in decades, and has continued its downward course since. The days of easy volume growth were over. In all honesty, global beer consumption increases have been a phenomenon of a handful of very large countries and regions and AB-InBev would have enjoyed most of the windfall. Its major emerging market is Brazil, where per capita consumption is approaching developed-world levels (68 litres per annum versus 76 litres in the US). For another, there was a tectonic shift to contend with. An affliction hitherto only registered in mature markets appeared to have caught on in major emerging markets too. Across the globe, consumers have been increasingly drawn to beers that skew either to the high-end or the low. Brewers responded by raising prices and launching high-end products but these have failed to compensate them for declining sales of their mainstream brands. AB-InBev is no exception. It may have more than 200 beer brands in its global portfolio, yet it has always focused on the biggest ones, the 16 that have retail sales of over $1 billion each. Among them are Bud Light, Budweiser, Corona Extra, Skol, Brahma, and Antarctica, all mainstream brands in their countries of origin. It was time to remember the adage: If in need, clinch a deal.

One more for the road

In the early days of globalisation, highfaluting strategy messages were used to justify major transactions, Mr Brock's feeble one being an exception. Curiously, nowadays, there are none forthcoming and, what's more, no one seems to mind. Although the $100 billion SABMiller takeover, dubbed MegaBrew, will be the third-largest deal in history, AB-InBev's offer in 2015 was termed – modestly, it appears – 'Proposal to build the first truly global beer company'. Only a pedant would object. Had not AB-InBev and SABMiller already billed themselves as 'global brewers' before? So, what is the difference between a 'global brewer' and a 'truly global brewer', except for an emphatic adverb that was most probably added by an over-zealous PR person? Of course, AB-InBev would not brag about wanting to create a beer behemoth with perhaps 400 brands, which would control about 30 percent of global beer volumes before disposals, and perhaps 50 percent of the beer profit pool. This Mr Brito left to the media to figure out.

Nonetheless, there were pertinent reasons why AB-InBev went after SABMiller when it did. AB-InBev has been losing its fizz. Global profits dropped in 2015 for the first time in years. Its two main markets, North America and Brazil, face a slump. This was the downside of AB-InBev's dependence on the Americas for its profits. While the going was good, the near total reliance on markets between Patagonia and Alaska for its EBITDA (86 percent of its global profits) was a boon. The American continent features some exceptionally profitable beer markets, above all the US and Brazil. Together with Mexico these three markets alone account for 75 percent of AB-InBev's profits. Three countries with a few big brands each should not have posed too many operational challenges, really. This has allowed AB-InBev to achieve extremely high margins; much higher than Heineken's and Carlsberg's and meaningfully higher than SABMiller's as well.

Once the going got tough, it became a different matter. Old Europe and China are no cash machines and Africa did not figure on AB-InBev's map. Already in 2015 Deutsche Bank delivered a critical verdict that AB-InBev's growth prospects looked dim. As Deutsche Bank said in a report: 'AB-InBev's embedded volume growth profile is considerably behind Heineken and SABMiller, with Mexico providing the much needed upside.' If AB-InBev's salvation lay with Mexico alone, it was time to roll up another company. Fortunately, SABMiller was available, unlike Heineken and Carlsberg, ranked third and fourth, which are backed by loyal shareholders (the Heineken family and the Carlsberg Foundation respectively).

If we accept that a company's price is indicative of the buyer's hopes for its future, AB-InBev anticipations rest firmly on Africa. SABMiller earned almost a third of its profits in Africa, where AB-InBev's sales are negligible. Analysts agree that Africa is the last continent where beer consumption will go up, and strategically its role is to replace Asia, which over the past decade has driven global beer volumes. But the good days in Asia are over, and in China in particular per capita consumption has reached Asian norms, which are far lower than Europe's.

Over the next decade Africa is forecast to provide 40 percent of global volume and profit increases. Growth will not be smooth; in Africa it never is. But, unlike China in the last 20 years, Africa's volume growth will be very profitable. When comparing China's annual beer production in 2015 (471 million hl) and Africa (141 million hl), the difference is stark. Sub-Saharan Africa contributed \$3.1 billion to the global profit pool, China only \$1.4 billion (2015). Luckily, most of Africa's markets are monopolies or duopolies, which should help ensure sustainable profits.

In addition, AB-InBev would get SABMiller's Latin American businesses, another major profit generator for SABMiller. Despite the steep price tag, which translates into an eye-watering 17 times EBITDA, or thereabout, and exceeds Anheuser-Busch's, SABMiller was cheap. Its share price had slumped between 2014 and 2015 because of a weak South African rand and Colombian peso. In other words, it was now or never for AB-InBev.

Thanks to AB-InBev's proven knack at rolling up companies, slashing costs and lifting value, bankers were more than willing to write out cheques. AB-InBev has said it will strip the acquired assets to the order of 'at least $1.4 billion' a year in annual running costs by 2020. SABMiller's executives would have made sure that, by industry standards, SABMiller is pretty lean, much leaner than the old Anheuser-Busch had been. Given the Brazilians' track record of under-promising and over-delivering on their cost-cutting targets, Mr Brito will have to squeeze the new assets until the pips squeak.

The takeover has been very drawn out, projected to drag on for a year, since AB-InBev made it dependent on securing regulatory approval beforehand. In order to placate the beady-eyed anti-trust cohorts, AB-InBev committed itself to dispose of certain SABMiller assets. The first to go was SABMiller's stake in the US joint venture MillerCoors. It was sold to Molson Coors for about $12 billion. AB-InBev has further got rid of the Grolsch and Peroni businesses to a keen and eager Asahi for a couple of billion dollars. All things considered, AB-InBev was probably lucky to offload SABMiller's 49 percent in China's Snow Breweries, to the state-backed majority shareholder China Resources Beer, for $1.6 billion. Originally analysts had expected the stake to fetch $5 billion, but in view of China's beer production nosediving and rising competition, AB-InBev must have felt glad it got that much. At the time of writing (August 2016), AB-InBev was seeking a buyer for SABMiller's central European businesses, including the Pilsner Urquell brand.

While AB-InBev has let it be known that these disposals were meant to soothe regulatory concerns, we believe that the Brazilians were actually glad of the excuse to cut out a lot of dead wood as they had done after the takeover of Anheuser-Busch. They decided to part with SABMiller's businesses that did not live up to AB-InBev's criteria of straightforward growth prospects. This applies to SABMiller's so-called 'global brands' Grolsch and Peroni, which were surplus to AB-InBev's requirements as they paled in significance (read volumes sold) next to Budweiser, Corona and Stella Artois. The same holds true for SABMiller's central European units. This leaves a question mark hanging over SABMiller's stakes in Castel, the privately-owned French brewer in Africa, and in Anadolu Efes, which operates in Turkey, Ukraine and Russia. Most observers concur that AB-InBev would be daft to let go of the former, whereas it might like to get shot of the latter, which faces all kinds of issues in its territories. What will become of them, we shall see.

On the whole, the Brazilians have cleared the regulatory hurdles pretty well. They had even anticipated some wobbles following the Brexit vote, which weakened the pound. Almost casually, they lifted their cash offer by £1 per share from £44 a share to mollify SABMiller shareholders who had grumbled they would get less once they converted the pay-off from their sterling-denominated shares into another currency.

In our view, the takeover of SABMiller was both a reaction to the changing geography of beer consumption, and an attempt to counteract a slow decline in consumption. Killjoys said this did not add up to a compelling case for investment, but for the Brazilian roll-up it did. It needed to continue growing, cost what it may.

The consequences for the whole industry are significant. This is the endgame – the last meaningful takeover in the brewing industry and it makes the Brazilians the undisputed leader. Even if Heineken and Carlsberg were to merge, which is unlikely, they would fall short of MegaBrew's size. Jointly they might control perhaps 15 percent of global beer volumes and profits. In the Beer Monopoly their status is now that of also-rans.

What are the prospects for the big brewers? The short answer is: not terrible but no longer fabulous.[31] That's why we believe that AB-InBev will be planning its next coup already. In April 2016 it set itself an ambitious goal: $100 billion in turnover by 2020. This will be a stretch. The combined AB-InBev and SABMiller will have a turnover of $66 billion, minus disposals. AB-InBev will have to either make another big acquisition or gee up revenues considerably. Even if Africa were to witness phenomenal consumption increases over the next few years, the target will still remain beyond AB-InBev's power without another deal.

In his critical assessment of AB-InBev, Mr Cuadros says that the Brazilians' blueprint for growth resembles creative destruction without the creative part. They strove to claim a bigger piece of the pie rather than making the pie larger.[32] He underestimates that their blueprint for taking over stable businesses with high margins and large market shares to increase profits is creative, only in a different way. It is quite an accomplishment to repeat the triple jump – takeover, cost-cuts, profit increase – over and over again. Mr Cuadros may bemoan the fact that the Brazilians have made a travesty of progress by unilaterally equating it with profit hikes. Again, he fails to see that this is what roll-ups, that are in thrall to finance capital, have to do. They are not 'addicted' to clinching deals as *The Economist* claims, they are merely following a finance-led logic. We are sure that Mr Lemann will have a plan for the next takeover. After all, bankers are already placing bets on it.

SABMILLER: THE GRAHAM SHOW

It beggars the imagination and runs counter to our image of big corporations as ocean tankers, silos or psychic prisons. Is it really possible that the two-decade-long rise from a middling market player to a global brewer with 70,000 employees in over 80 countries was planned and orchestrated by merely three people? In the case of SABMiller, the answer has to be a resounding 'Yes'.

At the time of writing (summer 2016), the world's number two brewer, SABMiller, is in the process of being taken over by the world's number one brewer AB-InBev. In a few months' time it will – officially – be no more. Although it pains us for various reasons to see SABMiller go, this is exactly what these three men foresaw when they pushed their South African company onto the international scene.

The three men are: SABMiller's long-time CEO, the late Graham Mackay, who passed away in 2013, its Executive Chairman Mayer Kahn (1990–2012), and its Chief Financial Officer Malcolm Wyman (2001–2011). Of course, to do his achievements justice, one should add Norman Adami, who insiders ungraciously called Mr Fixit because in his 35 years with the brewer (until 2014) he led the reversal in fortunes, firstly of Miller Brewing in the US, which the group acquired in 2002, and secondly of the brewer's unit in South Africa, after Heineken severed ties with SABMiller in 2007 by terminating the very profitable licence for the Amstel brand.

What these three or four men did, in the words of one competitor, was to 'form a consistent and capable management team, which pursued a well thought-through strategy with an endgame in mind.'

To better understand the full extent of their achievement it should be rephrased thus: When Messrs Mackay, Meyer Kahn and Wyman decided to use the window of opportunity opening up after the dismantling of apartheid in 1994 to take South African Breweries (SAB) international, they had already grasped the fundamentals of Beer Monopoly: buying individual streets or markets would get them nowhere. They needed the monopoly of all the street of the same colour (in their case Africa) to move on to the next stage – globalisation. Knowing full well that their position in the Beer Monopoly was precarious since they were a listed company without any dedicated shareholders providing a safeguard from takeovers, they immediately understood they lived on borrowed time: they could only do lunch until they became someone else's lunch.[1]

That they might end up as AB-InBev's target one day might have dawned upon them in the late 1990s while vetting their fellow players in the game: who would be as shrewd as they were? At the turn of the 21st century there were only two: Belgium's non-risk averse Interbrew and Brazil's high-aiming AmBev, which had just been formed through the spectacular merger of the country's two largest brewers. When AmBev and Interbrew combined in 2004 to take over Anheuser-Busch in the US and AmBev finally revealed its true colours as a roll-up company, their resolve must have been: make AB-InBev pay for the most expensive high roller lunch ever in the brewing industry.

Did they play the Beer Monopoly right? Obviously. After 20 years of unparalleled beer consumption increases, the times of easy volume growth are over. Unsurprisingly, AB-InBev gave as its compelling rationale for the deal with SABMiller: '[The] African continent would be a critical driver of growth for the combined company, building on the strong heritage of SABMiller in the region'.[2]

A brewer in a pariah state

In order to flesh out the argument, this chapter will trace SABMiller's ascent from a market leader in a pariah state[3] to a truly global company. It made Mr Mackay not only one of the longest-serving corporate leaders[4] in the brewing industry but one who also served his shareholders well. Between 1999 when he became CEO and 2013, the time of his death, SABMiller's stock rose 1,000 percent on the Johannesburg Stock Exchange.[5] As Mr Mackay used to say, his performance review as CEO of SABMiller was simple, and available for everyone to examine: the company's share price.[6]

Born in 1949, Mr Mackay was brought up on farms in Swaziland, Natal and Rhodesia (now Zimbabwe). His father was an itinerant farmer who lost his own farm but moved around to manage farms for others.[7] Young Mackay graduated as an engineer in 1977 before joining SAB as an IT Manager in 1978. According to SABMiller's official biography, he quickly moved over into SAB's management, rising through the ranks to hold a number of senior positions in the group including his appointment as Executive Chairman of the beer business in South Africa in 1992.

An *uitlander* without political goodwill

By then, SAB, as the company was called before changing its name to SABMiller in 2002, was already a long-established company, having been founded in Johannesburg in 1895. But 'long established' should not be taken to mean that SAB enjoyed political goodwill, the kind of boost which launched its peers into the world. SAB has had to confront all kinds of major political, cultural and social issues in the 20th century, not least because of the deep fault lines between Anglos, Afrikaners, coloureds and blacks in South Africa. We should not forget that following the Boer War (1899-1902) the Union of South Africa was only established in 1910 after the peace treaty of Vereeniging when the four provinces of the Cape, Oranje Freistaat, Transvaal and Natal came together. But the country remained under British control until 1948.

To the outside world, South Africa may have appeared British, but inwardly it was dominated by Afrikaner nationalism. The National Party was the governing party from 1948 until 1994. Its policies included apartheid and the promotion of Afrikaner culture, whose origins are Dutch Calvinism. For most of its history SAB had to face up to accusations in South Africa that it was an *uitlander*, a foreigner. It listed on the London stock exchange in 1898, which in the eyes of the Afrikaners made it a British-domiciled and -owned company. Until the 1950s, over 80 percent of SAB's shareholders lived in the UK. As cultural prejudices tend to die hard, SAB deemed this bad for business. When the brewer approached the UK parliament for permission to change its domicile to South Africa, it was rejected. Defeated, it asked the South African cabinet to transfer its domicile, but got a chilly reception. Only in 1970 or 1979 (sources differ)[8] was SAB incorporated in South Africa. However, by then 80 percent of its shares were in South African hands.[9]

Straddling a segregated market

It may seem utterly callous to put it this way, but from the point of a brewer set on growth, the South African beer market proved an uphill struggle as regulations and culture provided strong headwinds. Until the early 1960s, most South Africans, or 70 percent of the population, were under prohibition. In 1928, a ban on the sale of European liquor had been introduced for black people. This racially inspired prohibition remained in place until the Afrikaner-dominated wine industry managed to sway the government to give it access to black consumers. In 1962 the Liquor Laws Amendment Bill came into effect and black South Africans were allowed to buy liquor freely again. The end of prohibition did not make South Africans rush for a beer. As the Afrikaner government had always favoured wine over beer, in 1971 European-style lagers ('clear beer') represented only 9 percent of the total alcoholic beverage market; the far cheaper opaque sorghum beer dominated at 49 percent, with wine, brandy and other tipples making up the rest.[10]

In effect, SAB had to straddle a segregated market as it aggressively took over all of its local competitors and waged battle with those that refused to succumb, while securing vertical integration and building large state-of-the-art breweries to keep costs and beer prices down. SABMiller's mantra, 'to drive the company to be bigger, better and more profitable', was coined by Dick Goss, who was just 38 years old when he took over the helm at SAB in 1968.[11] Before many northern hemisphere brewers seriously thought of cost control, SAB was already ruthlessly slashing its own. Not because SAB was greedy for profits – it always strove to maximise them – but because in an emerging market the price of beer is the major obstacle to volume increases. Mr Mackay later admitted: "Even in the depths of apartheid, when the country was isolated, we still would travel the world comparing our operating practices with those we found overseas, and studying how the Americans ran their wholesaling system, how the Germans ran their quality. There was benchmarking all the time."[12]

It was the corporation's ability to harness the social consequences of apartheid that provided the key to the success of their brewing operation and gave it a market share of nearly 99 percent at the end of the 1970s. This alone would have made SAB a nice and secure company to work for, especially if you happened to be male and interested in beer and sports. But SAB and its people had to tread carefully, both politically and economically. Under apartheid, the 1980s proved a difficult time and South African businesses found themselves caught between a rock and a hard place. The South African economy was faltering. They could neither attract foreign investments nor expand outside their home turf. In 1986 the Western anti-apartheid campaigns had successfully persuaded the US Congress to pass the Anti-Apartheid Act, which prohibited bank loans to South Africa and banned the importation of a number of South African products. Other countries followed suit. Thus South Africa saw itself pushed into diplomatic, economic and cultural isolation.

Conglomerisation by default

Apartheid affected SAB strategically, one consequence being that the brewer was forced to invest much of the cash from its highly profitable beer business into industrial and retail assets, ranging from supermarkets, clothing, shoes, furniture, and matches, to plate glass and hotels, which all performed poorly in comparison with beer. As SAB became a conglomerate other South African companies did likewise – and SAB fell victim to what was called a hostile takeover. In 1983 three major shareholders, the miner Anglo American, Johannesburg Consolidated Investment Company, and the insurance company Liberty Life, clubbed together and established a holding group, Premier Group, whose combined shareholding gave them control of 34 percent of SAB.

SAB's leadership was not amused. It had not been consulted and an angry Dick Goss resigned. The shareholder putsch may have irked SAB's leaders at the time but it became a real worry in the next decade. By 1989 Premier Group had put the SAB stake into a new vehicle called Bevcon, which was put up for auction in 1999. Guess who showed an interest? US brewer Anheuser-Busch. In her book *Dethroning the King* Julie Macintosh gives an insider's account of the meeting between August Busch III and Graham Mackay in London which ended after a few minutes with Mr Busch leaving the room. He had wanted full control of the whole company – more than Mr Mackay was prepared to grant – and refused to compromise.[13] In the end, this tie-up withered on the vine and SAB managed to purchase 10 percent of its own shares following the unbundling by Bevcon of its entire shareholding in SAB. The lessons Mr Mackay and his team would have drawn from the convoluted Bevcon story are these: They needed to find more malleable and reliable shareholders if they wanted to take part in the globalisation of the brewing industry, and they had to gain access to foreign profit streams.

Should I stay or should I go?

The opportunity arose in 1994 when South Africa had its first democratic all-race elections and apartheid peacefully rather than through a revolution – as had been feared – came to an end. In retrospect, it seems that Mr Mackay and his team were at the ready. Whether they were apprehensive that the new black government and its left-leaning politics would throw the country into turmoil, or whether it was the consolidation of the international brewing industry about to begin that made them rush into foreign fields – whatever the case, SAB's disadvantages in that it lacked both capital and a big brand with global potential were easily overcome by smarts.

"I'm telling you," [Mr Mackay] once told his team at SAB, "we don't need to have an inferiority complex about being South Africans … I'm telling you that we can conquer the world." "A lot of people doubted us," said SAB's Mr Adami, "but we had a lot of self-belief. I don't think it was arrogance. It was conviction, and that came from Graham."[14]

SAB unchained

Having missed the early stages of the internationalisation of the brewing industry for intrinsic reasons (as an export brand Castle never had the pull of the Heineken or Carlsberg brand) and political circumstances (the international boycott of the apartheid regime), Mr Mackay quickly adopted the 'buy and build' tactic to expand overseas. In the 1990s, SAB's strategy rested on three pillars. Firstly, they would join the game and acquire cheapish assets in Africa, China and the newly opened markets in eastern Europe. Because of their intimate knowledge of the South African beer market, Mr Mackay and his team thought they knew how emerging markets ticked. Given the correlation between population growth and rising GDP in the context of political stability, beer consumption of affordable mainstream brands would only go up from very low levels. Benefitting from the forecasted organic growth seemed like a no-brainer.

The second strategic decision was to restructure SAB from a conglomerate to a more focused brewer and get rid of the loss-making parts like OK Bazaars. The supermarket chain was sold in 1997 for a symbolic one rand. The third resolution was to get access to western investors, who previously would have shied away from putting their money into an emerging market player for fear of the associated risks. These missions had their high points in 1999 when SAB listed on the London Stock Exchange and bought the Czech brewer Pilsner Urquell.

Getting his house in South Africa into order, Mr Mackay effectively had to undo all his predecessors' work of diversification and return SAB to its roots as a beer and beverage company. Selling off the unwanted bits was a massive challenge, remembers David Williams, a media commentator. 'The execution was a jewel of managerial craftsmanship, but in many respects not noticed because of Mackay's serenely confident but understated style. To describe Mackay's leadership in cricketing terms, he was like a batsman who always saw the ball a little before everyone else did. He always seemed to have time.'[15]

Push into Africa

True, it was the South African unit which served as the company's engine room, both in terms of money and personnel – about 200 executives were expatriated over the first ten years – and which fired up SAB's expansion into Hungary, Poland, Romania, Slovakia, the Czech Republic, Russia and China. However, these were then fragmented markets and SAB's wished-for domination would take time and effort, as SAB's competitors were getting interested in these countries too. Not so in Africa. Many years later, analysts would talk of Africa as SAB's back yard, in much the same manner that the US refers to Latin America and Russia to the Ukraine – as if there was an analogy between the world of beer and the world of geopolitics. Besides, Africa was not foremost on SAB's mind in the early 1990s. Nonetheless, ten years later SAB was producing one third of all beer in Africa and enjoying monopolies in many of its markets, albeit often through management control only.

'In the mid-1990s, it got onto something of a roll in its African expansion by acquiring several newly privatised national breweries in Zambia, Tanzania, Mozambique and Uganda.'[16] In 2014, *The Economist* ran a story on SABMiller's expansion into Africa with the subheading 'A long-established African firm went global, only to find the fastest-growing market was on its doorstep', insinuating that SABMiller's African conquest was opportunistic rather than strategic. In the article, Mark Bowman, at the time head of SABMiller's Africa division, admits that his company's rapid expansion was somewhat unplanned: 'at this stage it was about fixing the companies.'[17] In other words, the breweries were mostly going cheap, and SAB brought know-how and sounder management with the unambitious intent of simply making these companies turn a profit.

A one-stop shop

Opportunistic these African ventures may have been, but they were never regarded as incidental. As Mr Mackay said, 'you cannot be a real country without a beer or an airline.'[18] Africa's beer markets were predominantly monopolies, which immediately gave the buyer the number one position and market control, not least through its dominance of logistics. These aspects alone served to keep potential competitors away. All the monopolist brewer had to do was to grow consumption by offering local beer brands at the right price and the profits would keep going up. Mr Mackay understood this only too well, having developed the blueprint in South Africa. That is why, in a presentation to South African shareholders in

1996, SAB's Chairman Meyer Kahn put up just one slide and spoke on it for more than an hour. The slide showed a map of Africa. The thrust of his message was: 'Africa is ours.'[19]

Of course, Africa has never been wholly SABMiller's. But it succeeded in becoming the major brewer in Africa, despite its late start, because it was quick on its feet and outpaced its competitors when opportunities arose to buy into a market. The drinks group Diageo (Guinness beer), Heineken and France's Castel Group have been busy brewing beer across Africa far longer. However, once they saw that SAB had entered into a market, they wisely stayed away from it. It was as if by silent agreement they would honour the others' monopolies. Observers attribute SAB's deep penetration of its African markets, many of which are relatively poor and some are Muslim, to Mr Mackay's other insight: these markets needed an integrated beverage approach.

This meant turning SAB into a total beverage company, offering malt beer, sorghum beer, carbonated soft drinks, and bottled water in more affluent countries and, perhaps, just soft drinks and water in the poorest. Recognising that there is an endemic problem in Africa of toxic home-brew consumption, SAB investigated whether it was possible to produce beer from the cheapest and most widely grown form of starch on the continent, cassava. In 2011, the group launched a commercial clear beer from cassava called Impala, which was only marginally more expensive than the dodgy brews thanks to tax benefits, and it became wildly popular.

Africa boosters and Africa doomsters

Our guess as to why SAB has never bragged in the media about its involvement in Africa, a market of 1.2 billion people, is that its leaders would have known that western investors are prone to extreme mood swings when it comes to Africa. In the past, for every Africa booster there were several Africa doomsters, who would take turns in out-shouting each other, depending on whether commodity prices were rising or falling. What is more, an emerging markets brewer whose main source of revenue was other emerging markets was considered a risky investment in the 1990s and certainly did not draw the kind of enthusiasm from analysts as it did in the Noughties. The acronym BRIC only made its debut in a 2001 report by bankers at Goldman Sachs, when the four nations it referred to – Brazil, Russia, India and China – made up just 8 percent of the world's total economy. But for more than a decade, the assumption that the BRIC countries (and later the BRICS, including South Africa) should be treated as a linked economic force, representing the rise of emerging markets, drove billions of dollars in investment decisions from fund managers and consumer goods companies.

No doubt, in the late 1990s, the Africa doomsters ruled the roost just as SAB was to seek a secondary listing on the London Stock Exchange. The move was politically risky as many in South Africa thought that SAB was doing an unpatriotic runner, remembering SAB's original UK listing in the 19th century, thus undermining confidence in the ANC government. 'These sensitivities had to be carefully handled, and nobody was more adroit at doing so than Mackay, supported by Meyer Kahn ... and Norman Adami.'[20]

Fear and loathing in London

The South African journalist Ann Crotty remembers: 'Mackay and fellow directors Malcolm Wyman and Meyer Kahn were adamant they needed access to the sort of better-priced funding that came not just with a London listing, but with inclusion in the FTSE 100. It was a choice of remaining a very big fish in a small Johannesburg Stock Exchange pond, and inevitably being an early victim in the consolidation process [of the brewing industry], or quickly establishing a credible and defensible position on the FTSE, which could be used to bulk up its business and fund a predatory strategy.'[21]

Initially, they thought that entering the FTSE 100 ranked 85th was comfortable enough. Then came the collapse of the rand, which was the currency for 85 percent of SAB's earnings, and they feared that SAB would be evicted from the FTSE 100, perhaps leading to the company being ignominiously taken over.

In the pivotal year of 1999, the trio must have suffered from many sleepless nights: they had to worry over Bevcon's move back in South Africa, their future in London's FTSE 100, and their chances of success in the Czech Pilsner Urquell auction. Few people doubt that Mr Mackay felt rushed to buy a brand with international clout. Not only did SAB not have one while its peers all did, he also knew that in times of slow beer consumption growth (total beer production worldwide climbed by a scant 1.5 percent in 1998), affluent consumers would still splash out for an aspirational brand. Mr Mackay got lucky and Pilsner Urquell, regarded as the world's original lager, was his for $630 million.

Becoming SABMiller

By 2000, the internationalisation of the brewing industry was over and globalisation, with its own special rules – trans-continental deals among competitors – kicked off in earnest. Looking on from the sidelines, observers noted that the globalisation of the brewing industry seemed to defy previous financial logic, as there were hardly any synergies to be had when combining beer businesses which had no geographical overlap. But in those days everybody learnt as they went along. And SAB embarked on a quick learning curve.

Next on the list for SAB was the purchase of Miller Brewing (49 million hl beer), the number two brewer in the US with a 19 percent market share, in 2002. This transaction, while answering to the rules of the Beer Monopoly of trans-continental deals, had a certain defensive element too. Mr Mackay saw that SAB continued to be vulnerable to a takeover. The whole London media scandal, involving the leaked 'Zulu' documents from Belgium's Interbrew about a raid on SAB in 2001 underlined that the trio had plenty of reason to fear.

It was not as if SAB had sought out Miller, although SAB and Philip Morris had been talking for years. The returns that SAB could expect from such a combination were so small that Meyer Kahn once famously quipped that he would rather buy government bonds than a brewer in a developed market.[22] The reason Miller came on the market was that its owner Philip Morris, nowadays called Altria, the maker of Marlboro cigarettes, was refocusing on tobacco and was looking for a buyer for its beer business. It was not hard to see that Miller was badly run. Its market share had dropped to 20 percent compared with Anheuser-Busch's 49 percent – and its brand Miller Lite, which pioneered the light beer category in the 1970s, seemed in perennial decline. Not that Philip Morris did not care. In the 15 years prior to SAB taking over Miller, there had been seven turnaround plans and almost as many management changes at the top, albeit to little avail.[23]

The takeover of Miller

However, Mr Mackay thought he could make this deal work, especially since Altria, for tax and other reasons, 'wanted to be paid in scrip and not in cash' according to Mr Mackay.[24] Other brewers would have balked at the suggestion. But this served Mr Mackay and Mr Wyman, a former investment banker, just fine. They did not have to spend any cash and still got control of a first-world brewing company with a dedicated shareholder to boost. The transaction, valued at $5.6 billion, was structured so that Altria received a 36 percent stake, since diluted to 27 percent, in the new company called SABMiller, while SAB took on about $2 billion of debt held by Miller. Some observers called the deal a reverse takeover because Philip Morris became SABMiller's biggest shareholder. So what? The South African trio had dealt with unpredictable shareholders before and, compared with Bevcon, the cigarette maker Philip Morris looked as solid as a rock.

The Miller acquisition turned SABMiller into the world's number two brewer and gave the business a wider investment base. Henceforth, SABMiller was taken more seriously by US investors, as the US was and is the largest beer profit-generating market in the world. At first, Mr Mackay probably thought they stood a good chance of turning Miller around. They deployed Mr Fixit, Norman Adami, to Milwaukee with the mandate to stop the decline in sales and market share.[25] Mr Adami certainly succeeded in revolutionising the 'Socialist Republic of Miller', which did not challenge employees to perform, and he managed to woo disgruntled distributors to support Miller again. Alas, no matter how hard he and his team tried, raising market share in the US remained an elusive goal. At least Mr Adami succeeded in knocking the market leader Anheuser-Busch off its game. In 2005, Anheuser-Busch's operating income fell 22 percent, its first such decline in a decade. Analysts reckoned that Mr Adami was a key factor in the $10 billion decline in Anheuser-Busch's market capitalisation between 2002 and 2005,[26] which would have made Anheuser-Busch's leadership chew their ties – had they worn any.

Ever the long-term strategist, Mr Mackay would have set his eyes on a follow-up deal early on that would get him ahead in the US: a link-up with the US brewer Coors. The brewer of the eponymous beer brand had found itself in an equally tight spot. Ranked number three with a market share of merely 12 percent, Coors would have struggled to improve margins and profits. The opportunity to set up a joint venture with Coors arose in 2007. This did not stop Mr Mackay from testing the waters with Anheuser-Busch and InBev at the same time.[27] Nor did it prevent him from taking a closer look at Scottish & Newcastle.

Weighing his options, Mr Mackay chose Coors. The deal, which combined Miller's presence in the Midwest, where

Coors was typically soft, with Coors' relative strength in the western US, created a new entity, dubbed MillerCoors, with a 29 percent US market share – Anheuser-Busch remained number one at 49 percent – and a net revenue of about $6.6 billion. The transaction was supposed to deliver $500 million in cost savings within three years. Shrewdly putting vanity behind strategic benefits, Mr Mackay did not object to Leo Kiely, previously CEO of Molson Coors, becoming CEO of the joint venture, although the Miller business was bigger and SABMiller had a 58 percent stake in the joint venture.

Commenting on the joint venture, Mr Mackay said that it provided an excellent opportunity to rationalise their businesses. In actual fact, it could not have happened at a better time, as it led to much-improved profits all the while the US beer market declined and craft brewers embarked on their meteoric rise.[28] What Mr Mackay did not say was that the deal had barely been agreed when InBev took over Anheuser-Busch. Without the joint venture SABMiller would have found itself faced with an even more formidable competitor in the US than the old Anheuser-Busch had been.

Colombia's Bavaria: a landmark deal

With the battle between SABMiller and Anheuser-Busch in the US garnering so much media attention in the Noughties, it is easily forgotten that SABMiller clinched three more major deals in that decade. It bought Italy's brewer Peroni in 2003, Colombia's Bavaria in 2005, and the Dutch brewer Grolsch in 2008.

The years 2002 to 2007 were among the busiest in the brief history of globalisation. In its annual report 2007 SABMiller says: '[The past five years] saw a steady flow of mergers and acquisitions, with the bigger brewers the busiest. Over this period, the top 20 brewers have been involved in more than 280 deals with a total transaction value of over $80 billion. Activity has been particularly heated in emerging markets where most of the brewers have made investments.' Thanks to various mergers and acquisitions the top five brewers accounted for 38 percent of the global beer market in 2007.

In our opinion, Bavaria was the landmark deal for SABMiller in that it had everything going for it. Never mind Colombia's international reputation as the biggest narco-paramilitary state in the Americas during the Noughties, Bavaria provided a well-run business, sizeable profits and a market where beer consumption was forecast to go up for years to come. SABMiller had beaten Dutch brewer Heineken in the race to buy Bavaria, which was then Latin America's number two brewer at 30 million hl beer compared with AmBev's 70 million hl and the world's tenth largest. Like most prized assets in emerging markets, Bavaria had monopolies in Colombia and several neighbouring countries through controlling stakes in leading brewers in Ecuador, Panama and Peru.

The acquisition of Bavaria was considered to be one of the last good opportunities for a large foreign player to tap into the Latin American beer market, among the most lucrative globally. Unlike China, which promised high growth in volumes but delivered low profitability, Latin

America, impressively, showed growth in both volumes and profits. SABMiller in July 2005 took a 71.8 percent stake in brewer Bavaria for $7.8 billion before buying an additional 25.2 percent for $1.2 billion in a tender that left it owning 97 percent. SABMiller paid for Bavaria in its preferred mode: stock and cash. According to rumour, SABMiller offered less than Heineken, but SABMiller was willing to structure the deal in a way that appealed to the owners, the Santo Domingo family, who wanted to retain some control over the combined group. The Santo Domingos, who had allegedly married SABMiller 'for beauty not for money', got a 15 percent stake in SABMiller (called BevCo), making them the second largest shareholder behind Altria.

The advantages of the deal immediately showed. By helping to create a wide and balanced global spread of businesses between mature and emerging markets, Latin America became SABMiller's second most profitable market region behind South Africa, contributing nearly $1 billion or 25 percent to group profits in its financial year 2007, although South Africa still provided the bulk of earnings at 33 percent.

Family brewers cashing out

When comparing the stakes both Altria and the Santo Domingos got in SABMiller for their respective dowries, one is struck by the discrepancy. Although the Santo Domingos brought a far more profitable business to the table, they ended up with a much smaller stake. Were they hopeless at bargaining? Or was there consensus between the South Africans and Altria that the Colombian market was fraught with higher risks than the relatively stable US beer business and the Santo Domingos did not merit a better deal? Whatever the reasons, the impression remains that the Santo Domingos were treated less favourably than Altria.

In contrast to the Bavaria takeover, SABMiller's other two deals in the Noughties – Peroni and Grolsch – appear like aberrations from Mr Mackay's clever globalisation strategy. Analysts certainly voiced their disapproval when in 2003 SABMiller paid – in cash – a total of $640 million to buy out Peroni's four controlling families over a period of five years. Everybody seemed to agree that SABMiller had overpaid for the maker of 'pizza beer', which then produced 4.4 million hl beer annually. Ranked as Italy's number two brewer behind Heineken, Peroni was not an effectively managed business and analysts fretted over whether SABMiller really had the therewithal to put Peroni on track while it was still struggling with Miller over in the US. The consensus among investors was that the acquisition made neither financial nor strategic sense, and that SABMiller was spending money merely for the sake of it.

There is no question that the Peroni family had timed their sale well. Like other family-controlled brewers that put themselves on the block in the Noughties, they knew that a lot of cash in hand was better than a trickle of prospective dividends, especially when they saw their attractiveness to acquisitive global brewers dwindle fast as these potential buyers began to set their sights on far bigger deals. There were at least five other family-controlled brewers which sought a rewarding exit: Germany's Beck's, which was sold to Interbrew in 2001 for $1.6 billion; Munich's Spaten, that went to Interbrew in 2003 for about $550 million; Germany's Holsten, controlled by the Eisenbeiss family, that was acquired by Carlsberg in 2004 for $1.34 billion; the Dutch brewer Grolsch, in which the de Groen family held a 37 percent stake, that was sold to SABMiller in 2007 for $1.2 billion, and Mexico's Grupo Modelo with the Corona Extra brand, which was offered to AB-InBev in 2013 for $20 billion.

SABMiller and Peroni: entering high fashion

In 2003, SABMiller had to beat off competition from some of Europe's largest brewers, including Interbrew, Carlsberg and Scottish & Newcastle, to acquire Peroni and gain its first production foothold in one of two western European markets where beer consumption was actually growing – the other one being Spain –, albeit from a very low level. Italy's beer consumption stood at 29 litres per capita compared with a western European average of 75 litres.

So where did SABMiller see beauty in Peroni that eluded its critics? It would have been Peroni's export brand Nastro Azzurro, since renamed Peroni Nastro Azzurro, which had established export positions in markets like the UK, the US and Australia.[29] Although SABMiller owned Pilsner Urquell, it would have come to realise by then that the Czech Pilsner was actually a bit of a dowdy brand that did not quite enjoy the global pull Mr Mackay believed it did when he bought it in 1999. So SABMiller decided to elevate the lifestyle brand Peroni to trophy brand status, next to

Pilsner Urquell, because it thought it needed a euro brand to keep its US distributors happy. In those days, sales of premium import beers in the US were growing at 5 to 6 percent per year.

It helps to remind ourselves of the rapid succession of deals in the Noughties. At the very same time that it was entering into a joint venture with Coors in the US, SABMiller was in hot pursuit of Grolsch. Whereas the US joint venture made strategic sense, clinching a deal with the Dutch in November 2007 followed a far baser but no less comprehensible motive: spite.

Tit for tat

In March that year, Heineken had terminated SABMiller's licence to manufacture and distribute Amstel lager in South Africa with immediate effect. This meant a loss of $300 million in revenue and $80 million in annual profits for SABMiller, or 2 percent of SABMiller's 2007 profits. Additionally, it wiped 9 percent off its market share (2.3 million hl), which subsequently dropped to under 90 percent in South Africa. Business-wise, the loss of Amstel was a major problem. SABMiller suffered an instant decline in market share in the premium segment, which had grown over 20 percent in 2006, in a national market up just 2 percent. Worse still, it did not have an international brand that could match Amstel in consumer appeal.

The licensing agreement with Amstel was first signed in 1965 and had been renewed several times over the course of the next 40 years. However, it always represented a liability for SAB, and Mr Wyman admitted as much when he said in 2007 that SAB and Grolsch had been in talks for seven or eight years before the Dutch were amenable to a sale.[30] As a 3.3 million hl company Grolsch did not come cheap. SABMiller had to fork out – in cash – $1.2 billion, which represented an 84 percent premium to Grolsch's share price. Despite the high price tag, this time analysts did not grumble that SABMiller had overpaid. They understood Mr Mackay's argument that the brewer needed this brand to roll out across Africa and Latin America in pursuit of growth. In the second half of the Noughties, sales of premium beers were rising nearly three times as fast as mainstream and economy brands globally. In addition, as investment bank JP Morgan wrote in a 2007 report, premium brands generated a profit per unit often double that of non-premium brands.

SABMiller responded to the loss of Amstel by accelerating the marketing and sales of premium and imported brands such as Peroni and Pilsner Urquell. Mr Mackay knew this was not enough to recoup profits and market share, since Heineken had announced it would attack SABMiller directly by building a brewery near Johannesburg, which would become operational in 2010. Therefore, in 2008, Mr Mackay persuaded the recently retired Mr Adami to return to his old job in South Africa, where his approach to addressing the competitive challenge was to squeeze out costs so as to make up for the loss of the Amstel profits, which were then reinvested into brands and enhanced route-to-market practices. This way disaster was averted. In 2015 SABMiller's market share in South Africa was still only 90 percent, but its local profits had risen to $1.9 billion from $1.1 billion (beer and other beverages) in 2007. Luckily, for SABMiller, Heineken's South African venture began badly and seems not to have been thought through, especially when Heineken decided, to much consternation, to mainstream Amstel, robbing it of the premium image South Africans were used to. Over the years SABMiller's Castle Lite took up much of the market segment and by 2015 Amstel was a shadow of its former self.[31]

Chances missed and taken

The last opportunity to buy into the Latin American market came up in late 2009 when the families that controlled the Mexican brewer FEMSA Cerveza (Sol, Tecate, Dos Equis), put the company up for sale in an auction. FEMSA Cerveza had operations in two of the world's six biggest beer markets, being the number two player in Mexico and a distant number four in Brazil. Both SABMiller and Heineken were interested in buying FEMSA, with SABMiller initially seen as the front runner. But Heineken was very determined not to lose out to SABMiller, as it had done in 2005 with Colombia's Bavaria, because Heineken already had an agreement with FEMSA to distribute its beers in the US up to 2017.

None of the bidders was afraid to be number two to Grupo Modelo, which dominated in Mexico with a market share of 57 percent and was at this stage part-owned by AB-InBev through its takeover of Anheuser-Busch. It was an open secret that AB-InBev would eventually seek to acquire the other half in Grupo Modelo it did not yet own, and competition would seriously heat up. No, the main stumbling block, according to media pundits, appeared to be price. FEMSA was said to be looking for close to $10 billion for its beer business, while SABMiller and some analysts thought a price around $7.5 billion more realistic. FEMSA was doing well in Mexico, but its Brazilian unit was loss-making. In December 2009 SABMiller bowed out of the bidding, allegedly because it believed FEMSA's value was closer to $7 billion. This way Heineken came to clinch the deal in an all-share transaction that valued FEMSA at $7.6 billion.

Family ties

Some found it strange that SABMiller, having the balance sheet strength for a big deal, walked away when the difference in valuation between them and Heineken was a few hundred million dollars and when FEMSA got exactly what SABMiller had previously offered to Philip Morris and the Santo Domingos: a stake in the enlarged group.

Small wonder that analysts griped that SABMiller had fallen behind in the globalisation race, passing up the chance to buy Scottish & Newcastle in 2008 and now FEMSA Cerveza. Meanwhile, InBev had taken over Anheuser-Busch. By comparison, SABMiller's last mega-mergers were with Bavaria in 2005 and Miller as far back as 2002.

Insiders say that SABMiller really did not stand a chance of getting FEMSA. The chemistry between the Heineken family and the FEMSA people was undeniable. In other words, Heineken was willing to give FEMSA a major say on its board as second-largest shareholder with 20 percent of stock, while SABMiller was already diluted through other major blocks of ownership. To its own detriment, SABMiller stubbornly refused to raise the price.

Mr Mackay would not have been too pleased that he had lost out with the Mexicans. Fortunately another opportunity to buy big already loomed on the horizon: Australia's number one brewer Foster's, which would come on the market in 2011 and which would be expensive – over $10 billion to be paid in cash. Media said SABMiller had been courting Foster's for some time. Since 1993, Miller had been the marketing and sales partner for Foster's in the US, taking over the brewing rights in that market in 2007. Plus, in 2006, SABMiller acquired all of Foster's assets in India, including the licence for the brand. Not content with that, SABMiller had been trying hard to break into the Australian market, a duopoly between Foster's and Lion, by acquiring the minor Bluetongue brand in 2007, and building a new brewery through Pacific Beverages, its joint venture in that market with the local bottler Coca-Cola Amatil.

Australia's beer profit pool beckons

Luckily, SABMiller was the only bidder for Foster's, as several of its competitors were too stretched financially to be able to consider such a large deal. On the face of it, Foster's did not fit SABMiller's original predatory pattern, which focused on brewers in emerging markets. Like Miller before, Foster's was a first-world brewer in a market where beer consumption was in decline. A large chunk of Foster's profits came from selling imported Corona Extra – a licence, everybody knew, that would be revoked as soon as SABMiller's people walked through Foster's doors and given to Foster's rival Lion, owned by Japan's brewer Kirin.

With or without the Corona licence, Foster's was a high-margin business. After all, in 2011 Australia's beer profit pool on sales of about 17 million hl beer was larger than China's with sales of an enormous 490 million hl beer. For SABMiller, the rationale for the deal was mainly about running Foster's better and more efficiently. Analysts estimated that the combination could produce some $150 million in cost savings per year. Compare that with Foster's alleged profits from the Corona licence – $65 million in EBITDA – and it's easy to see why SABMiller was not too fazed by having to relinquish this brand. In his famous dead-pan fashion Mr Mackay acknowledged at the time: 'Foster's has an enviable portfolio of local brands and that's where there's been some undermanagement.'

It must have been around the time of the FEMSA sale that analysts began to tout the endgame scenario and wondered when AB-InBev would take over SABMiller. This deal had been on the cards since the mid-2000s, when it was rumoured that Anheuser-Busch was InBev's Plan A and a tie-up with SABMiller InBev's Plan B. As we found out in 2012, there were meetings between InBev and SABMiller to discuss a merger as early as 2007. However, discussions foundered because at the time InBev was unwilling to pay a significant bid premium and favoured a merger, while SABMiller was uncomfortable with the strong controlling position of InBev's core shareholders in any potential merger and felt that they could not sell such a structure to their shareholders.[32] Therefore InBev chose to pursue Plan A and bought Anheuser-Busch instead. Once AB-InBev had this transaction and the follow-up one with Mexico's Modelo – announced in 2012 but only completed in 2013 because of complex anti-trust issues – wrapped up, the takeover of SABMiller became a question of when, not if. After all, AB-InBev was already looking around for targets. In the brewing industry, there were only a few companies that caught its eye – and the biggest was SABMiller. Heineken was family-controlled, Carlsberg was in a world of trouble with its exposure in Russia, so this left SABMiller as the most viable target.

The sale

In 2012 the *Wall Street Journal* published an article about CEO Mackay moving to the position of SABMiller's Executive Chairman for a year before taking on a non-executive role after the departure of long-standing Chairman Meyer Kahn. Though this was in defiance of corporate governance rules, SABMiller justified his promotion on the grounds that Mr Mackay's role was to support the new CEO, Alan Clark.

Prophetically, the article was entitled 'SAB Shuffles Deckchairs on the Titanic',[33] which you could interpret as implying it was a pointless manoeuvre soon to be overtaken by events. However, what the *Wall Street Journal* failed to mention was that SABMiller's leadership already felt the clock ticking away and decided they would need an old hand at dealmaking – Mr Mackay – when AB-InBev came knocking. However, in December 2013 Mr Mackay passed away and the first half of 2014 went by without AB-InBev making a move.

This was just as well, as it gave SABMiller the opportunity to appoint to its board a new heavyweight dealmaker, the South African Jan du Plessis, in August 2014. Insiders noted that Mr du Plessis would sport two hats: one as Chairman of SABMiller, and another as Chairman of the British-Australian miner Rio Tinto, indicating that SABMiller was awaiting an offer and that Mr du Plessis' job was to make sure SABMiller's shareholders got the best deal out of AB-InBev.

Poker-faced SABMiller

In a cunning move, and probably in an effort to force AB-InBev's hand, SABMiller's CEO Mr Clark began talks with Heineken about a takeover. In the past, brewing industry bigwigs were always in talks about deals, as the episode between Mr Mackay and August Busch III shows. These discussions were conducted behind closed doors and all participants agreed to keep shtum if they remained inconclusive. So why did Heineken make public in September 2014 that it had received and rejected a takeover approach from SABMiller? Was this seemingly embarrassing rejection in SABMiller's interest? Definitely, as they would have known that the Heineken family would never agree to a takeover. But SABMiller's executives were in a hurry. Throughout the first half of 2014 SABMiller's stock had risen and then begun to decline in June as no offer materialised. It was now or never for SABMiller; the lower its share price dropped, the cheaper SABMiller would be for AB-InBev.

SABMiller's stock continued its downward slide in 2015 until mid-September 2015. It jumped 20 percent in one day after AB-InBev had disclosed it intended to make a takeover approach. Talks dragged on for two months and proved Mr du Plessis to be a feisty negotiator. He not only triumphed in forcing AB-InBev to up its offer three times from the initial offer. He also managed to boost the board's morale, especially when it became known that Altria had already wanted to cave in. However, Mr du Plessis and the Santo Domingos convinced the rest of the board that AB-InBev needed SABMiller more than SABMiller needed AB-InBev. Mr du Plessis pushed his luck for another improved offer. In the end, an 'exasperated and frustrated'[34] Mr Brito complied, putting an offer on the table that added a 50 percent premium to SABMiller's stock when deal talks had first begun.

Who was to gain from the transaction apart from AB-InBev? Fortunately, this deal was clinched in London, one of the most gossipy financial centres ever. Nosy parkers would have had no problem finding out that an army of takeover experts would share a massive pay-out. The fees alone were estimated at $430 million to be split between three teams: AB-InBev's advisors ($120 million), SABMiller's advisors ($120 million) and the bankers ($190 million), in return for a record corporate borrowing package of around $75 billion.

SABMiller's senior managers were believed to do nicely out of the sale as well. Some 1,700 of the brewer's top executives will see shares and options vest which could be worth up to $2.1 billion. Mr Clark was allegedly in line for more than $65 million. For Mr du Plessis, it would have been a lucrative few months' work. Media said he is sitting on shares worth £1.3 million and will receive £650,000 for his brief chairmanship.[35]

And the winner is … Altria

Of course, the biggest winner from SABMiller's sale will be the tobacco company Altria, which is expected to accept a cash and stock offer, through which it will possibly end up with a 10 percent stake in the much-larger AB-InBev. Well done Altria and without any effort, to boot. Had Altria not sold Miller to SAB in 2002, Miller today would be ranked perhaps tenth largest global brewer, down six notches from 2000. Over the years Altria has done nicely out of SABMiller too. Annual earnings from its stake have grown from $600 million in 2010 to just over $1 billion in 2015, as the market value of its stake in SABMiller was hiked to nearly $28 billion in 2015 from Miller's original valuation of $5.6 billion in 2002. Compare that with what Molson Coors will have to put on the table for SABMiller's stake in the joint venture MillerCoors – $12 billion – which equals Miller's current value, and you can easily see that Altria made a clever decision when it took the passenger seat in SABMiller and let Mr Mackay do the driving.

Buy and build …

In the history books it will be Mr du Plessis who will be credited with having pulled off one of the biggest sales of the early 21st century. That he was handed such an attractive asset to sell is all due to Messrs Mackay, Meyer Kahn and Wyman. Acknowledging Mr Mackay's life achievement, Meyer Kahn said: "He had the foresight to see what the future held for the industry; he had the courage to join what we called the dance of the elephants."[36]

From our vantage point, SABMiller's rise through acquisitions looks ingenious. One insider summed it up thus: Mr Mackay was determined to push into emerging markets where others feared the consequences; he mainly looked for markets where SABMiller could achieve dominant positions; and, perhaps most cunningly, he avoided markets where SABMiller would encounter AB-InBev, which had two benefits – less competition and a long-term exit pathway.

It took some big egos, and not to say nerve, to plan and implement such a daring strategy. Mr Mackay was no shrinking violet. Nevertheless, he proved most adroit at forging partnerships, which ultimately provided SABMiller with 40 percent of its sales.[37] Mr Hansmaennel once criticised SABMiller for its reliance on 'growth through partnerships', which reduced its global empire to merely an assortment of bridgeheads. Well, this was Mr Mackay's preferred *modus operandi,* born out of necessity rather than inclination. Initially, his foreign acquisitions needed to be funded with equity (Miller, Bavaria) because he did not have the money for them. Only later, probably, did he see the advantages of such a network in that it would serve as a defence against predators. Still, it helped SABMiller's ascent to become the world's number two brewer with a well-balanced spread of operations between fast-growing developing markets and cash-generating developed markets. SABMiller may not have played Beer Monopoly to the extent that it controlled lots of streets of one colour but this is a moot point in view of its sales price, really.

… and add more value

For Mr Mackay, dealmaking would not have been a self-serving macho thing, despite the cloak and dagger thrills, the secrecy, the high drama. "What counts is what comes out at the other end," a German Chancellor once quipped. Same in the brewing industry. The Beer Monopoly, despite its emphasis on dealmaking, was equally about integrating the acquired firm and increasing the value of the enlarged company. As Mr Mackay frequently stressed, transactions would need to create 'more value', a higher profit than any sum paid.

Hence SABMiller preferred to buy into emerging markets and, where possible, acquire market leadership positions; due to lower competitive pressures, this offered higher profit margins than more fragmented markets with many smaller players. At the same time, its decentralised approach, hinging on the belief that beer is a local business where local brands resonate strongly with consumers, would have been instrumental in the growth of the business.

It might have even been advantageous that SABMiller lacked a flagship brand, analysts' complaints notwithstanding. Not having an eponymous brand ingrained in its DNA, SABMiller was free to develop its own business model whose tenets were to build local brand champions and achieve growth through efficient distribution and marketing. As long as the real action in emerging markets was in the mainstream segment, where local brands dominated and SABMiller could realise economies of scale, SABMiller's bottom line got bigger and bigger.

Making 1 + 1 = 3 work was not merely seen as an accolade for SABMiller's managers. It also helped hike SABMiller's overall value. A company's value is of utmost importance in stock-for-stock mergers, when no cash changes hand, and in a sale. In this respect, Mr Mackay's deft hand at creating more value through deals and the subsequent managerial excellence displayed by his people have served SABMiller very well in its exit. The numbers speak for themselves. In 2004, SABMiller's market capitalisation was £6.6 billion. In 2016 its value was £70 billion, which made it rank fifth (June 2016) among the biggest British firms on the London Stock Exchange, up from 34th in 2004.

Looking back, Mr Mackay's skill in courting and aligning different cultures – as proven by SABMiller's shareholder structure and business partners – has to be applauded first and foremost. On SABMiller's behalf Mr Mackay must have performed quite a few diplomatic juggling acts to keep all his various associates in line: Efes in Turkey and Russia, Castel and Coca-Cola in Africa, CRE in China, Coors in the US. Consensus would have often required some prodding. However, there were never any hints in the media that SABMiller and its partners had headed off to arbitration courts, as was the case with Mexico's Grupo Modelo, the industry most notorious wrangler, who often needed to solve its issues with partners in courts.

Several insiders have the utmost respect for SABMiller and what they achieved, especially in China, the graveyard of many a brewer's aspirations. In 1994, SABMiller was among the first to enter China, again through a local partnership. While many foreign brewers struggled and eventually beat a retreat, SABMiller's joint venture, CR Beer, in which SABMiller had a 49 percent stake, grew to become the market leader by slowly developing the then little-known regional brand Snow into China's first national brand. In 2015, the joint venture operated close to 100 breweries. Many competitors admire their ability to handle such operational complexity in an emerging market and hold a long-term vision in place that others only dreamt of. Undeniably, SABMiller's would have been a very long-term vision as, according to rumour, it took 18 years before they could pay themselves a dividend. Also, earnings from China might have been higher if the Chinese partner had allowed them to bring in their international trophy brands – which they would not.

Given SABMiller's intrinsic disadvantages in that it was a listed company and did not enjoy unwavering shareholder support like some of its competitors, it is an admirable achievement that SABMiller lasted as long as it did. Not prone to illusions of grandeur and invincibility, Mr Mackay and his team would have understood they lived on borrowed time. Nevertheless, he had the courage to join the dance of elephants. It is a sobering thought that all the while he was building up SABMiller Mr Mackay had to bear in mind how it could most profitably be broken up. But he would have known that playing Beer Monopoly also allowed for a number two, which would make its shareholders wealthy when sold. If this had been his plan, all we can say is: mission accomplished.

HEINEKEN: A FAMILY AFFAIR

Isn't this a classic TV sitcom plot? If you want to make someone who is apparently taking no interest to declare his undying love, you flutter your eyelashes at someone else. This is what must have been in SABMiller's mind when in September 2014 they got down on bended knee and made their proposal to Heineken. Their real strategy? They wanted to make AB-InBev insanely jealous.

Think of it: Why would SABMiller risk public humiliation if their heart was genuinely set on wooing Heineken? Feigning irritated surprise, Heineken responded by issuing a press statement, saying SABMiller's proposal was 'non-actionable' and that 'the Heineken family and Heineken's management are confident that the company will continue to deliver growth and shareholder value.'[1]

'Non-actionable' may be a strange turn of phrase for a rejection. But, for the record, Charlene de Carvalho-Heineken and her husband Michel de Carvalho expressed their annoyance with SABMiller in an interview three months later, revealing that SABMiller's top brass had informally proposed teaming up many times before, and Heineken had always responded with the clear message that they had no interest.[2] To seasoned armchair strategists it would have been as sure as eggs is eggs that the Heineken family would rebuff SABMiller. After all, hadn't the Heinekens over the past 150 years done everything to keep their family business independent?

The Heineken family, headed by the fourth generation Mrs de Carvalho-Heineken (born 1954), may not control the majority of shares in the brewer, Heineken N.V., but through a tiered holding structure it still determines its destiny.

Mrs de Carvalho owns 88.67 percent of the investment vehicle L'Arche Green, registered in Switzerland, which in turn has 51.709 percent of listed Heineken Holding (2015). The holding itself has a 50.005 percent stake in the brewer. Separately, Mrs de Carvalho holds a 0.03 percent stake in Heineken Holding. That way the family exercises leadership although its economic interest is only about 25 percent. Of course, there is a reason why Heineken's ownership structure is so byzantine, and it's to do with the brewer's chequered history. However, there has not been the slightest doubt, since Mrs de Carvalho took over in 2002 on her father's death, that she would never accept a takeover offer from a rival, regardless of price.

Family companies are an often-overlooked form of ownership. Yet they are all around us, from the mom-and-pop corner shops in our cities to the millions of small and medium-sized enterprises that form the bedrock of Europe's economy. Where a family owns a significant share and influences important decisions, these companies are best characterised as chasing long-term targets and pursuing a vision of the company as a legacy to be passed on. In this respect, the histories of the families and the companies are almost inseparably intertwined. Or, as Mrs de Carvalho put it: "As family we are part of Heineken's past, present and future."[3]

The obvious difference between private family companies and stock market-listed ones is that the former are not driven by concerns over pushing the share price up; their main objectives are a steady stream of dividends and keeping control. They are also guided by a deeply ingrained learnt-at-the-dinner-table sense of history and morality, best exemplified by the paintings of dour-looking elderly gentlemen in stiff collars that tower over successive generations at corporate headquarters, as if wanting to instil in their progeny a mortal fear of 'screwing up' (not our choice of phrase but Mr de Carvalho's).[4]

Since everything hinges on family members performing to the best of their abilities, these companies tend to face unique challenges once they progress from their entrepreneurial beginnings. Only if they manage to combine a solid business performance with a resilient governance structure, and make arrangements to protect the family's reign in perpetuity, can they avoid the usual doomsday scenarios: quarrels over money, nepotism, disputes with the board, and infighting over succession. Although some family companies have miraculously survived for centuries – the oldest is said to be the Japanese temple-builder Kongo Gumi, founded in 578 and currently run by the 40th generation of the Kongo family – less than 30 percent of family businesses makes it to the third generation. As the saying goes, 'it is only three generations from shirtsleeves to shirtsleeves.'

In many ways Heineken was very nearly no exception to this rule. It was Gerard Adriaan Heineken (1841–1893) who started the business and took the radical decision that the future of beer consumption was not in traditional top-fermenting ales but in those brighter bottom-fermenting pilsner-type beers. It was the second generation, his son Henry Pierre Heineken (1886–1971), who nearly lost it all, and it befell to the third generation,

Alfred Henry 'Freddy' Heineken (1923–2002), to extract the brewer from the clutches of outside shareholders and self-interested board members. The fourth generation, Mrs de Carvalho, was not off to a good start either. By the time of her father's death, the brewer had lost out in the globalisation race, as disapproving analysts pointed out. While Interbrew and SAB had clinched big deals, Heineken had rested on its laurels as the best-selling international beer brand, watching growth stall and the share price decline. Fortunately, Mrs de Carvalho, her husband and their chosen CEO, Jean-François van Boxmeer, set to work quickly and put Heineken back on track again, so that today it ranks as the world's number two brewer.

Although in the following we will trace the brewer's past, our aim is not to give an abridged version of Heineken's comprehensive and lavishly produced corporate history, *The Magic of Heineken.*[5] Instead, our aim is to show how in family companies each generation adds their share of advice to the company's unwritten textbook on how to run a business. Put differently, it is to underline how in family companies contingent personal experiences and decisions are turned into timeless maxims.

The first generation – the age of brewers

The Heineken story begins, then, with Gerard Adriaan 'G.A.' Heineken. Seeking a strategic investment for the family's money, which he had inherited after the death of his father in 1862, he decided to put it into beer. Like Brazil's Mr Lemann more than a century later, he knew close to nothing about beer. But similarly to Mr Lemann, he would have thought that the beer business could not be very tough as he had heard of someone who had built a successful business on beer. Still, at the time it would have been a high-risk gamble. The idealistic Mr G.A. Heineken was betting the farm on beer becoming the new, less harmful, beverage of choice in due course. Way into the 19th century, Europe's poor had been grappling with gin addiction. As a matter of fact, alcohol consumption was a big social problem, particularly in the Netherlands, where people had taken to downing large quantities of cheap Dutch gin. Like many 19th century politicians, Mr G.A. Heineken would have been distressed by the gin craze and thought that beer, a wholesome beverage for the working man, would help wean people off Mother's Ruin, the contemporary slang for gin in England.

At the age of 23, Mr G.A. Heineken bought the De Hooiberg brewery in Amsterdam. He founded his company, Heineken & Co., and started selling beer in and around Amsterdam. However, since the 1850s new types of beers – Helles and Pilsner – had been imported into the Netherlands, both from Bavaria and from Bohemia. What made these beers different was that they were bottom-fermented rather than top-fermented, as was the case with the standard ales of his day. This resulted in brighter and clearer beers with a longer shelf-life – a prerequisite if beers were to be exported to far-flung places.

Only one year after taking over the De Hooiberg brewery, Mr G.A. Heineken, at the behest of the Amsterdam municipality, was obliged to move his brewery. He built a new one on the outskirts of the city in Stadhouderskade, which opened in 1868. Being a good Dutchman, who honoured traditions and kept a tight watch on his purse, he spent his money on equipment for producing top-fermented ales. However, he could not fail to notice the big increase in sales of imported lager beers from Germany; even while he carried on brewing ales, he grasped that a new trend was emerging, with people choosing to drink the more expensive pilsner that people called 'gentlemen's beer'. Today it would be considered a premium beer, as opposed to the top-fermented 'working men's beer' or mainstream beer. Wanting to find out what the German brewers were getting up to, he decided to send his trusted clerk to Germany to make the acquaintance of the German master brewer Wilhelm Feltmann, a colourful character who joined Heineken's new company in 1869. Furnished with an 'ambition and iron will' he would 'sweep the brewery up in the course of world history'. No false claims to modesty here by Heineken's historians Mathieu Jacobs and Wim Maas.[6]

In those days brewers did not think of technical innovation as a competitive advantage. Exploiting their friendly collegiality, Mr Feltmann had snooped around numerous breweries in Germany and Austria to study the ins and outs of pilsner brewing. Being in permanent contact with his boss, he was informed of the great success of the Viennese Dreher beer at the International Exhibition in Amsterdam. Mr G.A. Heineken, to his dismay, had to acknowledge that his beer was receiving little attention at the Exhibition. He therefore decided that if the market asked for a clear bottom-fermented beer it was time to produce it, and so he did, in January 1870.

Like any entrepreneur worth his mettle he had analysed the market, seen an opening and found a smart, technically adept brewer to help him. As the management guru Jim Collins would say in a modern context: he got the right people on the bus and got the right people in the right seats. Luck, in the guise of European politics, was also on their side, because of the 1870 war between France and Germany, in which the French army was defeated. As becomes a loser, French consumers took to boycotting all things German, especially beer. No slouch, Heineken stepped in, which led to a great increase in Heineken's sales of bottom-fermented beer in France. The sudden hike in demand was, however, unexpected and caused beer shortages in Amsterdam. Customers were angry. For Mr G.A. Heineken it was time to think about expanding brewing capacity. But where?

In January 1873 he incorporated Heineken's Bierbrouwerij Maatschappij N.V. (HBM) in Rotterdam, having decided to build a new brewery there on the grounds that a port might come in handy for exporting his beer. Unfortunately, news had reached him that another brewer in town, Oranjeboom, had had the same idea. Unfazed, he went to see the directors of the brewery and persuaded them to combine forces with HBM. The total share capital amounted to 1.2 million guilders, which was a hefty sum for relatively modest sales volumes. Mr G.A. Heineken held 70 percent of the shares and Oranjeboom the rest. The new brewery was dedicated to brewing pilsner beers exclusively for both companies. Production started in March 1874 and Mr Feltmann reportedly boasted that the days were over when all good beers came from Bavaria and Pilsen.

Gerard Heineken died in 1893, just before a shareholder meeting. His death immediately brought up the issue of succession. While fellow board member Mr Feltmann believed his own son would be the right man to head the company, Mr Heineken's widow, Lady Mary Tindal, who was now the major shareholder, decided to nominate her friend (and future husband) Julius Petersen as the new Director of HBM. Deeply disappointed that his widow wanted to keep it all in the family rather than sell her shares to him, Mr Feltmann fell ill and died in 1897.

These days, Mr G.A. Heineken is seen by some as a guiding light for entrepreneurship. Like his contemporary, the Danish brewer J.C. Jacobsen, the founder of Carlsberg, he provided his workers with decent workplace conditions; he took a measured risk; he invested in a superior quality product and in keeping his customers happy; he placed trust in industry innovations and he dared to think big (beer exports).[7] However, the other lessons that can be drawn from his story are more pertinent to family companies: without full control, negotiations over capital and profit allocations with the board and shareholders are a constant irritation, while a premature death can render succession plans problematic.

The task of growing the company fell to the second generation. Before Henry Pierre, 'H.P.' Heineken, probably Mrs Tindal's son from her affair with Mr Petersen,[8] became a director in 1914 at the age of 28, the company was managed by his mother and Mr Petersen. In the Heineken story, this would have been an interim period, which was dominated by labour unrest. The industrial revolution had made life wretched for the working class. Workers had banded together to form unions and campaign for change. Although Dutch workers were not as militant as the English, Heineken's board nevertheless judged it best to eventually concede some rights to its workers.

The second generation – stirrings of cosmopolitanism

Having obtained a doctorate in chemistry, Mr H.P. Heineken joined the board at a difficult time – the onset of World War I – and served as Chairman from 1917 until 1940. Heineken's historians describe him as an accomplished pianist, a cosmopolitan and a perfect team player. It would have been the last two characteristics which could help explain the company's new emphasis on expanding its international business. However, in Heineken's official history his role is somewhat downplayed when compared with those of his father and his son. This would indicate that he was a back-seat driver (team-player being a nicer term) who delegated the running of the business to two directors from outside the family, the export chief Pieter Feith and Dirk Stikker, a boardroom heavyweight, who more or less led Heineken between 1935 and 1948.[9]

Nevertheless, it would have been during Mr H.P. Heineken's stewardship that the company's export-based model was developed further. He and his team would lay the foundations for the 'build and brew' scheme: the gradual switch from exports to local production, which gave Heineken a head start in the internationalisation of the brewing industry. In retrospect it could even be argued that he pushed Heineken into Africa and Asia Pacific, which nearly a century later will still be set on growth when the rest of the world's markets will have turned flat or started to shrink. If this was his legacy, it surely cannot be surpassed.

With Dutch per capita consumption of beer increasing from 10 litres in 1919 to 28 litres in 1929, HBM's sales jumped from 182,000 hl to 611,000 hl in the same period. But the trend reversed in 1929 due to the world's economic crisis (The Great Depression) and the Dutch government increasing excise and tax on imported malt. Dutch beer production halved from 2.1 million hl in 1929 to 1.1 million hl in 1936. Heineken's own beer volumes dropped almost 50 percent, aggravated by a shift in consumption from the heavier German style beer that Heineken produced to cheaper and lighter lager beers. The sales of lager beers rose to 56 percent of total consumption in 1939. The decline in heavier beers hit Heineken particularly hard, and the competition from cheaper priced beers would have had Heineken's board having to consider the looming spectre of bankruptcy. Fortunately, the economy improved after 1936 and Heineken's sales picked up again, only to face another threat: World War II and occupation by the German Wehrmacht. Using local raw material sparingly, the Dutch breweries managed to survive the years 1939 to 1945. Due to the absence of other commercial beverages their weak wartime beers were much sought after.

Team work – the international expansion

At the beginning of the 20th century Heineken had established a profile abroad, but the board refrained from pushing export sales hard, considering them a high-risk strategy. After the death of their German export director in 1928 (who, bizarrely, refused to travel for business), this policy was changed under his successor, Mr Feith. Fighting a drop in consumption in their domestic market, the board had a change of heart and decided that beer exports would get special attention. At the time the country's colony of the Dutch East Indies – modern Indonesia – was Heineken's most important export market, although nothing would come of a plan to build a brewery on Java.

Disappointed by this failure, in 1931 Mr Feith was lucky to meet with representatives from Fraser & Neave (F&N) in Singapore. Founded by two Bible-peddling Scotsmen in the 19th century, the printing house F&N had branched out into soft drinks. The two parties hit it off, and in the same year they set up a joint venture and built a brewery, Malayan Breweries. Allocating tasks, F&N would contribute the capital plus distribution and Heineken the technical know-how.[10] It was a strategy which served Heineken well and allowed it to rapidly build and brew around the world.

With the US and Europe in the grip of the Great Depression, two European investment funds sought to benefit from rising beer consumption in resource-rich countries in South-East Asia and Africa. They were Gaston Dreyfus & Co, a French banking house with its subsidiary, Sofibra, based in Zurich, and the Société Internationale de Brasserie (Interbra) incorporated in Brussels. The two owned a string of breweries in nearly a dozen countries, from Morocco to French Indochina. Not wanting to be left out, Heineken had become a minority shareholder in Sofibra and Interbra.

But only after Mr Stikker spotted these hidden assets in 1935, and transformed the brewer's conservative accounting policy into a more dynamic one, could Heineken's position in these funds be reinforced. Once Mr Stikker had reorganised these disparate investments into a more integrated one, called Koloniale Brouwerijen (Cobra), with Heineken owning about 52 percent, the brewer enjoyed a far greater say in its foreign operations. According to Heineken's historians, 'HBM had been given a facelift and could now boast a worldwide image.'[11]

The house that van Munching built

After the end of prohibition in 1933, Heineken was the first foreign beer to arrive in the harbour of Hoboken, New Jersey. Was it luck or fate that Mr Feith had made the Dutch-born Leo Van Munching, who had worked as a steward on Atlantic liners, Heineken's US agent after their previous import company had floundered? In any case, after World War II he became their exclusive US importer and developed into a real asset to Heineken. He did not just know how to sell beer; he knew how to sell premium beer.

Thanks to Mr Van Munching's skill at wearing his clients down as he sang the praises of the Dutch beer's quality, Heineken's export sales to the US rose from 5,000 hl in 1936 to 11,000 hl in 1939. Business was tough during

World War II, and even more so in the immediate post-war years. Heineken's board repeatedly considered brewing its beer in the US, but after some debate the board always concurred with Mr Van Munching's reservations. Heineken beer would lose the goodwill it enjoyed with consumers overnight, and this insight has not changed. To this day, only imported Heineken is sold in the US.

In the 1950s sales to the US enjoyed double-digit growth, and Heineken was sold in upmarket hotels, restaurants and cafés. The price difference between a bottle of imported beer and a domestic brew was over 20 percent. In the import category, Heineken's biggest rival at the time was Germany's Löwenbräu, but Mr Van Munching was adamant that Heineken was the superior beer. Time proved him right, especially after Löwenbräu took the fatal decision to brew locally and rapidly lost its appeal. In 1958 Mr Van Munching celebrated his 25th anniversary as a Heineken importer. In truth, he was the brewery's largest single customer. The standard five-year contract had always been renewed but the ambitious Mr Van Munching began pressing for a contract in perpetuity. In 1960 forecasted sales of 60,000 hl were easily surpassed to hit 100,000 hl.

Intimidated by his bullish personality and mightily impressed by his sales figures, the board was cowed into awarding Mr van Munching a fabulous lifetime contract for himself and his son, Leo Van Munching Jr. By the end of the 1970s the Heineken brand sold 2 million hl beer in the US. In 1991, when Mr van Munching Sr died, sales were nearly twice as high. Heineken would have often regretted giving Mr van Munching a life-long contract, but the problem was solved by the intrusion of harsh realities. As soon as Mr van Munching Jr was presented with an inheritance tax bill of nearly $53 million he proved amenable to discussing selling back the contract, and Heineken jumped at the opportunity.

Expansion into Africa

It was in Africa that Heineken's internationalisation model fell into place quite neatly. The continent had long been an export destination for Heineken, with sizeable volumes being sent to British West Africa, including Ghana and Nigeria. In the colonialist era, Heineken's beer would have been consumed by the white elites. This changed after World War II as the British Empire began to crumble and more affluent local consumers discovered a taste for beer. Deeming political and economic conditions in West Africa extremely favourable, Mr Stikker and the British conglomerate, Unilever, agreed to build a 200,000 hl brewery in Lagos, Nigeria, for an estimated 2 million guilders (USD 10 million today). Unilever would be responsible for the commercial aspects, while Heineken had technical control. Both parties were minority shareholders (about 30 percent each) with the rest of the shares held by local trading houses. In 1949 the first batch of Star beer was brewed, and it turned out a more affordable alternative to the expensive imports. However, with an eye to their profits, Heineken decided to maintain a two track-policy throughout the 1950s: direct exports from the Netherlands as well as local production. This explains why in the mid-

1950s 50 percent of Heineken's exports – or one quarter of total production – was to West Africa.

By 1960, Heineken was exporting 100,000 hl beer to Ghana alone. All this came to a screeching halt when successive African countries gained independence and introduced protectionist taxes which priced imported beer out of existence. It was this unforeseen political event which made Heineken change gear and step up its 'build and brew' activities. Heineken quickly opened new breweries in Ghana, Sierra Leone and Chad. It also entered into co-operation with the Brasserie de Leopoldville in the Belgian Congo, now the Democratic Republic of the Congo, a company which became Bralima, with its well-known brand Primus. In 2015 this country was the seventh biggest African beer market behind South Africa, Nigeria, Angola, Cameroon, Ethiopia and Kenya.

The third generation – regaining control

As Heineken's international business grew, the family's situation became more desperate. Not only had Mr H.P. Heineken lost financial control of the family company when he floated HBM on the stock market in 1938 to raise money to pay a tax bill, he had also turned a closely-knit private company into a public one, which threatened to make HBM a plaything for the board and outside shareholders. Worse still, in 1940 he had had to relinquish his position as Chairman.

So grim was the situation that when the 25-year-old Freddy 'F.' Heineken returned in 1948 to the Netherlands (after a stint in the US with Van Munching to learn the tools of the trade and familiarise himself with marketing, a novel technique at the time for pushing up demand), he vowed that he would return control of HBM to the family. This was not just a vanity project. Rightly assuming that the Heineken name – both for the family and the company – signalled reliability to shareholders and customers alike, Mr F. Heineken wanted 'to prevent strangers from doing strange things under [his] name'.[12]

At his son's behest, Mr H.P. Heineken agreed to transfer his 45 percent stake in HBM to his two children. This did not appeal to the board, who had tried to keep Mr F. Heineken away from exercising his influence by giving him odd jobs at the brewery, like heading the ancillary advertising department. If this was not insulting enough, Mr F. Heineken had reason to suspect that board members were trying to make a grab for the company itself since they had already swindled his father out of his majority stake in Cobra. Therefore, in 1950, Mr F. Heineken set up Heineken Beleggings- en Beheermaatschappij (Heineken Investment and Management Company), HBBM for short, in which he deposited his minority HBM shareholding. On the quiet he also bought HBM shares, borrowing considerable amounts of money. It was a big gamble but worth taking since he had nothing to lose, having lost control of the company already.

Score, Freddy 2: Board 0

Plotting his next move, he was appointed to Heineken's Supervisory Board in 1951, taking over from his father, although working alongside the rest of Heineken's management could not have been easy. In 1952 it turned into an all-out boardroom brawl after he announced that he wished to become the Delegated Member to the Board of Directors, aka management. The board refused.

Mr F. Heineken retaliated in kind when in the same year he vetoed the board's plan to buy the Amstel brewery, Heineken's biggest domestic competitor. The cost of the acquisition, about 5 million guilders, would be financed by issuing new shares. To retain his majority shareholding he would have been forced to subscribe to 50 percent of this new issue with money he did not have. He rejected the transaction, thinking – rightly – that the Amstel deal could wait. Flexing his muscles, he threatened to have the board dismissed. A compromise was found: the board cancelled the Amstel transaction and Mr F. Heineken agreed to let the board remain in place.

By 1954 Mr F. Heineken's financial vehicle, HBBM, had acquired the majority of the brewer's shares, yet his personal debts amounted to a staggering 22 million guilders ($86 million today). Paying back his debt was something he would deal with in the future; his main goal had been accomplished. The brewery was again controlled by the family, and he had kept his promise to his father. It was time to raise his profile and influence within the company.

First, he applied his insight into advertising and marketing to the brand. He wanted Heineken to be a global brand like Coca-Cola. Clashing again with the board's conservative mind-set, which thought marketing a costly affair, he realised that the company had to change. In 1958, after six years of futile attempts, he was finally appointed Delegated Member, which gave him the right to veto decisions that did not suit him. Furthermore, he succeeded in giving the brewery a new constitution in 1960. The board of management was at the top of the parent company, HBM, with four independent companies below, each with their clearly defined tasks and responsibilities.

In 1962, he took the opportunity to offload his personal debt by floating the shares of HBBM on the stock market, of which 50.005 percent were acquired by his own Swiss firm. It's true that under him the brewer morphed into a strange stock market beast, with both HBM and HBBM being listed companies, but until the late 1990s this was considered a clever financial tool to raise outside capital without giving up control. In 1972, the brewery's name was changed to Heineken N.V. and HBBM's to Heineken Holding.

The company was finally ready for the future, with Mr F. Heineken as its boss. Having wrested power from the board, Mr F. Heineken chose to sit in the driver's seat. To this effect, he had himself appointed to the Board of Management in 1964 and to the position of Chairman in 1971 (until 1989). One of his first tasks was to abolish all the various Heineken labels that were in use around the world and replace them with a single one, thus securing a uniform global look, much in the same way as Shell and Coca-Cola had done. The next task was to consolidate the Dutch beer market and embark on a new round of 'build and brew'.

The takeover of Amstel

As we pointed out before, to play Beer Monopoly effectively, brewers initially have to secure a dominant position in their domestic markets; a simple lead is not enough. A market share of 30 percent is good, but 50 percent is even better. In the mid-1960s market share considerations dominated corporate thinking to such an extent that several Dutch brewers were looking to reinforce their positions through alliances with other brewers. They also hoped to counter the perceived threat from the founding of the European Economic Council (EEC) in 1957, a club of six continental countries which aimed at creating a common market. Heineken in particular worried that a foreign brewer would break into the Dutch market by buying a local brewer. Market shares were such that Heineken had 35 percent, Amstel 17 percent, while Grolsch and Oranjeboom had 10 percent each. What happened next was the Dutch brewers' version of ring-a-ring-of-roses.

Negotiations between Heineken and Oranjeboom came to nought in 1964 when Mr F. Heineken discovered that Oranjeboom was in contact with US brewer Schlitz. Next, Amstel and Heineken worked out a plan to jointly take over Oranjeboom, but they were rejected. To their surprise Oranjeboom decided to sell itself to Allied Breweries from the UK in 1967 for 51 million guilders ($15 million), or less than what Heineken and Amstel had offered. They subsequently turned their attention to the De Drie Hoefijzers brewery but were told that Allied Breweries had put 84 million guilders ($23 million) on the table. Heineken found itself in a real fix. With an acquired market share of 18 percent Allied Breweries would become a serious threat if they swallowed Amstel as well.

Spooked by Allied's swift progress, Heineken and Amstel entered into sales negotiations in 1968. In almost no time they hammered out a deal that valued Amstel at 150 million guilders ($42 million), a spectacular increase from the 5 million guilders a decade earlier. Although the companies' combined market share would top 50 percent (total volumes were 4.25 million hl beer per year), the Dutch government did not object, concurring with Heineken's claim that it was in the nation's best interest that no foreign brewer should obtain a leading position in the Dutch beer market. This line of argument would still sound convincing to the Brazilian government 30 years later, when it granted permission to Brahma and Antarctica to merge. The takeover of Amstel, although called a merger for the benefit of the public, fulfilled Mr F. Heineken's ambition: Heineken became the leading brewer in the Netherlands and got a second attractive brand, Amstel, thrown in as part of the bargain. In the 1960s the two brands accounted for 70 percent of Dutch beer exports.

Erecting Fortress Europe

Being a firm believer in the idea of a common European market – the European Economic Community was a precursor to the European Community and finally the European Union – Mr F. Heineken may have balked at the idea of having to compete with a foreigner at home. But this did not stop him from regarding the rest of the

EEC as Heineken's own backyard or, as he pompously called it, Fortress Europe. Looking at the numbers and the geography, Mr F. Heineken had concluded that Western Europe roughly matched the US in beer consumption. But conceding that there would never be a single beer brand for all Europeans, given Western Europe's strong national beer cultures, he pursued a hybrid strategy of 'build and brew' and 'buy and build' when entering these markets.

In the second half of the 20th century most European beer markets were fragmented; there weren't any national market leaders worth the name, let alone large national brands. This left Heineken with no option but to buy stakes in local brewers. Gradually over the years these stakes would be increased as groups were formed to lift market share overall. Ultimately, Heineken's various forays into Western Europe not only helped consolidate these markets; they also turned Heineken into a major player in France, Italy, Spain, Ireland, Switzerland and Greece, enjoying the benefits of broad market leadership (local brands) rather than just segment leadership (in the imported beer category).

Heineken's acquisitions track record in France best exemplifies Mr F. Heineken's internationalisation tactic. In 1972 Heineken acquired the Alsace group Albra, an association of four breweries. Their combined market share would have been less than 10 percent. In order to take it to 25 percent Heineken combined forces with the BGI group in 1984. In 1988 Heineken obtained full control of Sogebra and in 1996 of the Fischer group in Alsace with its famous Desperados brand. In 2000, the

French subsidiary Brasseries Heineken enjoyed a market share of 22 percent by volume and perhaps 30 percent by value, ranking number two brewer behind Danone's Kronenbourg. Kronenbourg was subsequently sold to S&N and ended up with Carlsberg after the takeover of S&N in 2008. Still, Heineken managed to gain market shares and become the leader – not least benefitting from the steady decline of Kronenbourg, whose beer sales have fallen from 11 million hl in the late 1980s to about 6 million hl in 2015.

Heineken's successes in achieving market leadership in several Western European countries notwithstanding, its stabs at internationalisation took time, often spanning several decades, with the desired outcome far from certain. If the goal was empire building, it proved inconclusive.

After the fall of the Iron Curtain and the disintegration of the Soviet Union new opportunities offered themselves in eastern Europe. Continuing the hybrid mix of 'build and brew' plus 'buy and build', Heineken ventured into Hungary in 1991 and took a stake in Komaromi Sörgyar. It bought into breweries in Slovakia and Bulgaria before entering the Polish market in 1994 by acquiring a small shareholding in the Zywiec brewery. Merging Zywiec with Mr Oates' Brewpole in 1998 initially made Zywiec the market leader, whose position, however, would be successfully challenged by SABMiller's Kompania Piwowarska.

Despite his visionary approach to consolidating the European beer market, Mr F. Heineken was a risk-averse, conservative leader. Relying on organic growth rather than on takeovers, he sought to internationalise his business with a steady hand. If this meant forsaking full control of a foreign company for merely the right to be heard, it was fine by him. Not hiding his disdain for the demands of other shareholders and for bankers, he insisted on internal finance to fund foreign acquisitions and on running Heineken his way. As he once said: "There are no specific targets I have to achieve in five years' time, nor do I have to ensure that profits rise by a certain percentage every year."[13]

Before retiring as Chairman of the Board of Management in 1989 he had invited his daughter Mrs de Carvalho to join the board of Heineken Holding. But he refused to relinquish control. "He had to be boss," recalls Mrs de Carvalho. "Delegating was not his thing."[14] This became more of a problem as Mr F. Heineken got older and became cautious and tightfisted. Popular psychology has tended to explain these character traits as the traumatic consequences of his kidnapping ordeal in 1983 – an assumption Mrs de Carvalho disputes. "I think he was just feeling slightly less king of the mountain."[15]

In 1990, Heineken was the world's number three brewer behind the two US giants Anheuser-Busch and Miller. In 2000, Heineken continued to rank third, but now behind Anheuser-Busch and Belgium's Interbrew. What had happened that this upstart Belgian brewer could overtake Heineken in under ten years?

Y2K hangover

The last decade of the 20th century marked the beginning of a new game. Internationalisation had run its course, and the race to 'buy and build' had begun. Tapping into external sources of finance, SAB and Interbrew had clinched ever bigger big deals on their road to empire. Following Mr Hansmaennel's roadmap, they strove to acquire significant market share positions in countries with sizeable profit pools – or at least with the prospects thereof. Globalisation was upon us in earnest in 1995 when Interbrew purchased the Canadian brewer Labatt. As Mrs de Carvalho later admitted, it was a mistake that in the bidding for Labatt Heineken had been too stingy and refused to make the concessions that Labatt wanted. Indeed, it proved a fatal error of judgement because other opportunities to take over a big North American brewer never materialised for Heineken.

There is no point in beating about the bush: by the time of Mr F. Heineken's death in 2002 Heineken was having a bit of a crisis. The brewer's profit growth had slowed, and the share price was declining. Relying on western Europe for nearly half of its profits and on the US for another 20 percent, Heineken earned only 15 percent of its profits from Africa and the Middle East, plus another 4 percent from the emerging markets of the Asia-Pacific region. In other words, Heineken's profit spread was unfavourably tilted towards mature markets. Under Mr F. Heineken, the brewer had upped its game in Europe alright. But as everybody knew, western Europe was a lost cause; all beer industry indicators pointed to a downswing. Making matters worse, Heineken had decided to give Russia a wide berth, leaving this boom market to its competitors for a carve-up.

Things did not look much better elsewhere. In the US, Heineken's star had begun to wane following the rise of Mexico's Corona Extra, which had already overtaken Heineken as the best-selling import beer. In Latin America, too, another big beer profit pool, Heineken suddenly found itself relegated to bit-part player, although this may have been because Heineken had got its fingers burnt after a failed brewery project in Venezuela during the 1950s and 1960s.[16] It only re-entered the continent in 1984 through a minority stake in Argentine brewer Quilmes. However, Heineken's position in Quilmes, the leader in southern Latin America, unexpectedly became untenable and had to be sold when Brazil's AmBev fully took over Quilmes in 2003. Farsighted remedial plans hatched by Heineken's board to buy the Andean heavyweight Bavaria, owned by the Santo Domingos, had been vetoed by Mr F. Heineken.

In Brazil Heineken was feeling a bit raw as its partner Kaiser – in which it bought a minority stake in 1983 – had faced all kinds of ups and downs, including a massive drop in market share. Fortunately the opportunity to acquire a stake in Chile's CCU arose after Heineken had joined forces with Germany's Schörghuber Group in 2001, or its presence in South America would have been reduced to a single wobbly bridgehead in Brazil.

Over in Asia, Heineken's decades-long partnership with F&N, Malayan Breweries, which was renamed Asia Pacific Breweries (APB) in 1990, had hit a rocky patch as the partners began to quarrel over strategy. To Heineken's frustration, F&N had wanted to push Tiger Beer rather than the Heineken brand and had proved nervous or downright reluctant to pour big money into China. Pursuing a pharmacist's approach to business, in the words of Mr Hansmaennel, which meant small volumes and high profit margins, APB's brewing capacity in China stood at only 1 million hl in the mid-1990s. It was a tiny drop compared with the huge pond of 150 million hl beer produced by Chinese brewers.

Hit by shareholder rebellion

Most worryingly, back home, Heineken's shareholding structure had come under attack by angry shareholders, who questioned the whole set-up of Heineken N.V. and Heineken Holding. The shares of Heineken Holding usually tended to trade at a 10 percent discount to shares of Heineken N.V., because chances of the Holding being sold were next to zero. By 2000 the gap had precipitously widened to over 30 percent. It had not helped that Heineken's CEO Karel Vuursteen had followed Mr F. Heineken's example and resisted pressure to improve shareholder value. An unapologetic Mr Vuursteen reportedly told American investors that he ran a company and did not manage the stock exchange.[17]

Some shareholders blamed the management of Heineken Holding and, implicitly, the family for this bad state of affairs. They demanded that Heineken Holding be liquidated, which was of course out of the question for the family. The reason for the widened discount was that several funds had sold their shares in small and medium-sized companies as they rebundled their holdings. But an activist investor pressed on and sought to have the matter settled in court. Fortunately, the 2001 hearing confirmed that the purpose of Heineken Holding was to secure the majority shareholding of the Heineken family and that shareholders in the Holding mostly bought their shares for dividends and not for speculative gains from share price hikes.[18] If the whole commotion served a purpose, it reminded the Heineken family that the brewer was not their private company which they could run in Mr F. Heineken's style by giving finance capital the cold shoulder.

The fourth generation – *prudenter agas …*

In the globalisation of the brewing industry, any corporate strategy was only worth the risk and the cost if it heeded a Roman's 2000-year old advice: '*Quidquid agis, prudenter agas et respice finem*', meaning 'Whatever you do, do it cautiously and look to the end.' Such was Mrs de Carvalho's inheritance that many in the industry thought she and her husband could only cash out or 'screw up'. She did neither. Honouring a moral obligation – a promise to her father – she would keep the business together until her eldest son was old enough to run it.[19] On her watch the family would not lose control of Heineken again. Although they had vowed not to meddle with day-to-day operations, Mrs de Carvalho and her husband nevertheless decided to shake up Heineken in four areas: the company's image with investors, its balance sheet, acquisitions, and the selection of board members and key executives.

The years 2000 to 2004 saw several major brewing industry transactions all with the aim of creating continental powerhouses: Carlsberg's joint venture with Orkla, S&N's takeover of Kronenbourg, AmBev's purchase of Quilmes, and Carlsberg's buyout of Orkla. Adopting the continental acquisitions pattern, Heineken in 2003 spent $2.0 billion on BBAG, the Austria-based brewer with leading positions in Austria, Romania and Hungary and smaller stakes in Poland and the Czech Republic. BBAG managed 22 breweries and sold about 13 million hl of beer. Combining with BBAG turned Heineken into the market leader in eight central European countries.

The takeover of BBAG, though compelling in its rationale of adding another piece to Heineken's 'Fortress Europe' jigsaw, did not win over the analysts. Nor did Heineken's venture into Russia, which many thought came far too late. In their defence, Heineken argued that they had entered Russia at the right time, when market forces had sifted chaff from the wheat, so to speak, allowing them to quickly acquire six groups with ten breweries all over the country between 2002 and 2006 for $1.5 billion. The financial markets still remained unconvinced, especially since Heineken's catch-up race in Russia awarded the brewer only a 16 percent market share in 2006 and a third rank behind Carlsberg and InBev.

Eventually the criticism hit home that Heineken had been sidelined by the mega-mergers that created SABMiller (2002) and InBev (2004) and was being out-manoeuvred in South America and China. Some of the blame for Heineken's lack of dealmaking was even attributed to the family's grip on the brewer, which had refused point blank to issue new shares in order to fund acquisitions.

Catching up

After witnessing Heineken's share price drop 30 percent between 2002 and 2005 and profits getting hammered by a plunging US dollar, forcing Heineken to issue profit warnings both in 2004 and 2005, Mrs de Carvalho was left with no choice but to resort to drastic measures. Her father's *Roi Soleil* days, when he could afford to ignore shareholder discontent and a sluggish share price that trailed behind its competitors, were gone. She had to put Heineken out of its misery and choosing a new CEO became top priority. Mrs de Carvalho and her husband urged the board to replace CEO Anthony Ruys with a more 'aggressive' leader, one who knew how to play Beer Monopoly.

Well aware of the tall poppy syndrome in corporations, which makes people reluctant to stick their heads up, they eventually settled on Mr van Boxmeer (born 1961), a Belgian, who had joined Heineken in 1984 and had led operations in the Congo, Poland and Italy. Widely regarded as more dynamic and reform-minded than Mr Ruys, Mr van Boxmeer was given *carte blanche* by the family to do whatever it took to clinch deals, raise profits and sway the analysts. As a banker, Mr de Carvalho understood only too well the new rules of the game. If you wanted to play with the big boys you abided by the tenets of finance capital. As he would say: "The best defence is always a high share price."[20] Not that Heineken feared a hostile takeover, but a high share price is nevertheless one of the prerequisites if you want to clinch deals and need to win over outside investors.

Reportedly, Mr van Boxmeer spent $28 billion on 49 acquisitions between 2006 and 2014, which extended Heineken's operations from 39 countries to over 70. Among those only three would warrant the title of 'landmark deal', in that they helped diminish Heineken's dependence on Europe by stretching its reach into up and coming emerging markets. All the same, only one transaction – the takeover of Mexico's FEMSA – genuinely fitted the pattern of 'buy and build'. The other two – S&N plus APB – were basically meant to rectify past mistakes and provide Heineken with full access to these firms and their markets. In effect, the purchases of S&N and APB were a tacit admission that Heineken's old ways of doing business through partnerships were fraught with far too many imponderables which could – and would – hamper growth.

In this respect, Heineken's acquisitions since the Noughties were not so much about embarking on a catch-up race in globalisation but an effort to strengthen its position. Ranking third among global brewers already, Heineken only had to expand quickly and calmly and clear up its act, while protecting the family's rule over the company. As the de Carvalhos and Mr van Boxmeer suspected, it would be an event beyond their control – the endgame when the world's number one brewer would buy the number two – that would work in their favour. Heineken would ascend to the number two rank. It was playing safe rather than hectic buying and building that guided Heineken through globalisation.

Here come the lager louts

When Heineken and Carlsberg jointly acquired S&N, Britain's last independent brewer, in 2008, the *Daily Mail* tabloid newspaper bewailed the fact that yet another British firm had become an overseas takeover target, this time by 'a bunch of lager louts at Carlsberg and Heineken'. Yet, nothing could have been further from the truth. Rather than striving to become a global beer champion, as the *Daily Mail* wanted to believe, S&N had prettied itself up for an exit. Its 250-year-old legacy notwithstanding, S&N was a hodge podge affair. It was the number one brewer in the UK, but until a few years earlier it did not even own the brands which were among its top sellers: Foster's Lager and Kronenbourg's 1664.

This state of affairs S&N sought to change when it got lucky in 2000 and snatched France's Kronenbourg away from Carlsberg. But it was only because the Foster's Group had staged a fire sale to fill a widening gap in its wine business that S&N was able to buy the rights to the Foster's brand in Europe in perpetuity in 2006. S&N liked to call itself 'a major European brewer with a balance of high growth emerging markets and high volume developed markets', even though the moniker 'European' had long lost its alluring ring and a balanced spread of risks appeared increasingly dubious. Fortunately, S&N had managed to gobble up some interesting assets on its way to the exit door: a stake in BBH (Russia), in United Breweries (India) and Chongqing Brewery (China). That's why it seemed like an attractive, albeit pricey target for Carlsberg and Heineken.

The takeover of S&N is one of the most interesting in the globalisation of the brewing industry as it highlights the fact that there were several ways to play Beer Monopoly successfully. S&N were looking for a profitable exit and got it. Carlsberg wanted S&N's participation in BBH, its business in China, plus Kronenbourg, to make up for its earlier failure. But what did Heineken see in S&N that eluded most eyes? That's a good question. Heineken got the Sagres brewery in Portugal, which is the market leader, but in terms of beer volumes Portugal is smaller than Ireland. It got S&N's tiny Finnish business and thus its first foothold in the Nordic countries, but the unit was sold again in 2013. It inherited the Maes brewery in Belgium, the number two brewer behind AB-InBev, which is far from being a money spinner because of its over-reliance on mainstream pils beer. It took on S&N's 37 percent stake in India's major brewer United Breweries with its famous Kingfisher brand and its equally flamboyant helmsman VJ Mallya, since accused of being a wilful defaulter after the collapse of his Kingfisher airline.

Stalling their competitors

Except for United Breweries these units would not have been much to write home about. For Heineken, S&N's most prized asset would have been its leadership in the UK, a market where Heineken had long struggled to reverse a decision made in 1969 when it granted the UK brewer Whitbread a licence to brew and sell a weaker mainstream version of Heineken at 3.4 percent ABV. The original plan had been to quickly gain a big share of the expanding lager beer segment, which grew from 5 percent in 1970 to

50 percent of the total beer market by the end of the 1980s. By then, however, Heineken's sales had begun to decline as people had gone off its watery beer. In a counter move, in 1985 Heineken decided to export the Dutch original to the UK under the brand name Heineken Export, which was positioned in the international premium segment. However, the pricier and more profitable international premium segment was already fairly crowded and dominated by Foster's, Kronenbourg 1664, Holsten, Carlsberg, and later by the 'reassuringly expensive' Stella Artois. Seeing that UK drinkers had developed a more sophisticated palate, Mr van Boxmeer called last orders on Heineken 3.4 in 2003 although it meant an immediate drop in sales volumes in the UK for the brewer.

Apart from leadership in the UK, thanks to S&N, Heineken also obtained the rights to sell Kronenbourg and Foster's in several countries. This minuscule detail would have escaped most observers. But it would have far reaching consequences: henceforth no one would wholly own the Kronenbourg 1664 and Foster's brands. Another international licence holder of Foster's was SABMiller, whose anxious quest for a global brand we outlined in the previous chapter. By getting the UK under its belt, Heineken effectively blocked or stalled its rivals' strategy to turn these brands into global ones. Incidentally, today Heineken sells as much Kronenbourg 1664 beer in the UK as Carlsberg does in France. This goes to show that you could even play Beer Monopoly obstructively. Whether this justified Heineken forking out nearly $7 billion was for others to decide. In the following year Mr van

Boxmeer described Heineken's performance in the UK as being affected by a 'perfect storm' with the economic slowdown and the ban on smoking in pubs taking their toll. The storm had not abated by 2012 when Heineken's Chief Finance Officer René Hooft Graafland confessed that the S&N acquisition was still behind schedule and had not reaped the expected returns.[21] Meanwhile beer consumption in the UK has continued its decline while competition between Heineken, AB-InBev, Molson Coors and Carlsberg has heated up. These days the only good news coming out of the UK for Heineken is the positive trend of cider sales – a segment in which Heineken is the market leader with the Strongbow and Bulmers brands.

Fortunately, financial markets tend to have a short memory, and Heineken's calamitous foray into the UK was forgotten as soon as rumours of its tie-up with Mexico's FEMSA hit the news in 2009.

Last chance cantina

In much the same way that AB-InBev pursued Mexico's Grupo Modelo, other brewers were eyeing up FEMSA Cerveza. Mexico has a large stake in the global beer profit pool and the country's two major brewers sport attractive brands. Rightly assuming that it was only a matter of time before AB-InBev would fully take over Grupo Modelo, Heineken and SABMiller began courting FEMSA. The trouble was, or not, that FEMSA did not want out. Although they had grown apprehensive of being isolated in the Americas with not enough bulk to compete with their larger rival AB-InBev, the Mexican families behind

FEMSA wanted in. In exchange for their 40 million hl beer business in the US, Mexico and Brazil, valued eventually at $7.6 billion, they requested a stake in an enlarged group.

This would have suited Heineken and SABMiller just fine. However, SABMiller could only offer the Mexicans a minority shareholding and less say than Altria and the Santo Domingos had. What's more, Heineken already had a contract to sell FEMSA's brands Sol, Tecate and Dos Equis in the US. Untangling this relationship and securing US anti-trust approval could have turned messy for SABMiller. Perhaps the Mexicans also worried what would become of them in the endgame of Beer Monopoly – if AB-InBev and SABMiller combined? It was highly unlikely that AB-InBev would be allowed to keep both Modelo and FEMSA and a total monopoly in Mexico. Preferring calculable risks to Russian roulette, FEMSA eventually consented to Heineken's offer, not least because Heineken's finance honchos had cleverly constructed the deal. The Heineken family would give the Mexicans a 12.5 percent stake in Heineken N.V., a 15 percent stake in Heineken Holding, plus two seats on the board. Nevertheless, this required a sizeable share issue by Heineken – the first time it had done so for an acquisition since it swallowed up Amstel in 1968 – and a commitment by the family to purchase shares which had to be handed over to the Mexicans within five years.

Capturing Heineken's upbeat mood, the *Wall Street Journal* ran a story in January 2010 entitled 'Fresh from a beer takeover in Mexico, Heineken CEO finds Davos refreshing. Goal of making Netherlands brewer a global force is well in hand'. Mr van Boxmeer and the Heineken family would have had every reason to feel upbeat. With the acquisition of FEMSA Cerveza, Heineken had finally created a platform for growth in three of the world's largest beer profit pools: in the US, Mexico and Brazil. Furthermore, in the Mexican families they had found themselves a partner who shared their long-term vision. And if the worst came to the worst, the Heinekens could always re-purchase the shares; the family's control would not be compromised.

Tanks in the streets

The same could not be said for Heineken's longest-running joint venture – the one with Singapore's F&N, their partner in APB. Heineken's plans for Asia could only be realised with F&N's consent, implying that Heineken could not act as swiftly and flexibly in Asia as in its fully-owned subsidiaries elsewhere. It may have rankled with Heineken that F&N insisted on prioritising Tiger Beer. Heineken's brands only made up around 30 percent of APB's volume sales but around half its profits. However, it would have nearly driven the Dutch up the wall that their frequently expressed desire to buy out the Singaporeans was always angrily swept aside.[22] Ownership of APB was complex. Jointly, Heineken and F&N controlled 65 percent of APB. Individually, they held shares in APB too. The relationship must have hit a low point in 2006 when F&N invited Singapore's state-owned investment fund Temasek to purchase a 14.9 percent stake, which was widely regarded as a means to fob off Heineken.

Despite clashes between the two parties, APB had grown to boast 24 breweries in 14 countries and produced 16 million hl beer in 2011. Ultimately, the battle for APB was unleashed in 2011 when Temasek sold its stake in F&N to Japan's Kirin. Naturally, Heineken was not pleased, but their hands were tied since Kirin was a competitor and a partner at the same time; they produce Heineken under licence in Japan. Deciding to grin and bear it, Mr van Boxmeer assured analysts that APB had succeeded in ringfencing Kirin from peering into APB's books. But in 2012 the alarm bells went off loudly after two Singaporean banks divested their stakes in F&N to a new interloper, ThaiBev, the maker of Chang Beer and Mekhong whisky and controlled by the Thai billionaire Charoen Sirivadhanabhakdi.

Barging onto the scene without warning, Mr Charoen had become the single largest shareholder in F&N, while his son-in-law had bought a 9 percent stake in APB. Not seeing that one coming, Heineken became panicky and moved quickly to acquire a controlling stake in APB. In August 2012, F&N's board accepted an offer from Heineken to acquire its stake in APB, worrying that Heineken would walk away with their brands if F&N backed a bid from another party. But a full-blown bidding war broke out when ThaiBev made a cash offer for all of F&N. The melee became even more chaotic after Kirin offered to purchase F&N's soft drinks and dairy business. It was tanks in the street. Eventually, Heineken struck a compromise with Mr Charoen. The Thais would support Heineken's offer for APB in exchange for Heineken refraining from bidding for F&N. The whole APB affair cost Heineken $4.6 billion. But it would have been money worth spending to close a chapter on a tumultuous partnership and to expand into Asia Pacific on their own terms.

... et respice finem

With their eyes firmly set on the endgame, AB-InBev became the world's number one brewer and SABMiller secured a profitable exit. In terms of strategic options, Heineken found itself in a league alongside Carlsberg. Because of their ownership restrictions, they only had a way in but no way out. Playing the exit card was out of the question. This marks the fundamental difference between investors and family owners. The ownership issue hampered Heineken and Carlsberg equally in their ability to raise the capital for takeovers.

However, Heineken fared better than Carlsberg. Looking to the end, the de Carvalhos and Mr van Boxmeer clinched several deals that gave Heineken a presence on all continents and access to major profit pools. Heineken may not hold many market leadership positions outside western Europe and Africa, for which they have the second and third generation of Heinekens to thank, but the family has still made the right moves in Beer Monopoly. They aimed at being the ultimate number two global brewer, which is a comfortable enough position and honoured by the financial markets, since competition requires at least two players. Not drawing anti-trust watchdogs' ire like AB-InBev, their options to do 'buy and build' in Latin America, Asia and Africa look far more numerous, especially after they quietly terminated their joint venture with drinks group Diageo in southern Africa and swapped assets in three continents in 2015. Indirectly acknowledging that the relationship with Diageo could turn into a rerun of the F&N saga, Mr van Boxmeer said that ending it was 'an important step' to 'optimally' structure the company's growth agenda.[23]

Unlike Carlsberg, Heineken's risk profile also looks more balanced. True, like Carlsberg and all the other big brewers, they were hit hard by the decline in the Russian beer market. Yet combining their units in Africa, the Middle East, Belarus and Russia in 2015 into their own version of an EMEA (Europe, the Middle East and Africa) region, a geographical mix common among North American companies and not considered untoward by investors, they turned the focus away from their struggles in Russia. Thanks to their profitable exploits in Africa, the whole region was set up to benefit them, numerically, that is.

In dealmaking Mr van Boxmeer showed himself an ardent follower of the 1+1=3 principle. Although no one in the industry would call Heineken a prime example of a scrimper, the brewer has assiduously reduced costs. Between 2000 and 2010 over 40 breweries and maltings were closed in Europe alone. If Mr van Boxmeer has stepped up his efforts in the past two years to cut costs, hike profitability and boost the share price, this would have been in an effort to satisfy investors. Being the number two brewer now, Heineken needs to compare more favourably with the huge profit machine that is the number one, AB-InBev.

What makes Heineken stick out in our quartet is that it still likes to do 'build and brew'. This marks it out as a brewer that does not shy away from entering markets the hard way by attacking local competitors head-on. In the past decade it has cracked SABMiller's monopoly in South Africa, it has faced up to Castel in Ethiopia and the Ivory Coast, while challenging Carlsberg in Myanmar. This tactic is not a fast track to empire building, but it underlines the fact that under Mrs de Carvalho the Heineken family has no intention of loosening its grip on the company nor that it needs to convince investors that Heineken's future looks rosy. At this point in time it's taken for granted, as is its desire to remain family-controlled. By continuing to go it alone, Heineken is preserving the family's heritage and profiting from it.

CARLSBERG: THE LONE RANGER

Summer 2016: Several anti-trust agencies have given the green light to the biggest beer merger of all times. Once the deal goes ahead, AB-InBev/SABMiller will drain most of the income from the global beer profit pool. In AB-InBev, SABMiller and Heineken, the global game of Beer Monopoly has found masterful players who do not just own Brazil Boulevard, Amsterdam Alley and Cape Town Crescent. Although ranked the world's number three brewer, Carlsberg seems left far behind. The hotels in St Petersburg Street and Kiev Avenue have a low occupancy rate. Beijing Lane and Tibet Road do not look much better either. With the SAIL '22 document, the hotel management has drawn up a plan for the future, but the strategy, 'Funding the Journey', is actually another austerity programme.[1] In the doldrums, the Danish brewer is trying to jettison ballast. The alternatives – raising more masts or unfurling extra sails – only seem to play a marginal role.

Carlsberg's current woes make it all too easy to overlook the brewer's impressive ascent. In the mid-1990s Carlsberg was one of the largest stock market-listed brewers in Europe, but investors deemed it boring, its management lacking imagination for further expansion. To many, Carlsberg was a conservative, truly Danish company, fully integrated into the concert of Danish business champions through cross-ownerships, a rotating management resembling a game of musical chairs, and supervisory board mandates. Uniquely in the brewing industry, Carlsberg was controlled by a foundation – the Carlsberg Foundation – to which father and son Jacobsen had each bequeathed their respective breweries, whose charter would serve as a poison pill for potential partners. In 1983, Carlsberg's CEO Poul Svanholm had said: 'We are not so interested in gaining sales by taking market shares from other breweries. That's not our way.'[2] This was probably with a nod to Carlsberg's foreign partners, who might have worried that they would get into bed with an untrustworthy and aggressive competitor. Mr Svanholm's dictum still seemed to apply a decade later, probably thanks to the staying power of the Danish beer cartel of 1903. But over time, deal fantasies could not be suppressed any longer and Carlsberg managed to acquire several property blocks in the game of Beer Monopoly. It was a phenomenon almost like Galileo's: 'and yet it moves!'

In many respects, Carlsberg begs to differ from its peers. Under the foundation's protection and safeguard it has trodden a Danish Sonderweg (separate path), determined by its roots and history. Carlsberg was founded in Copenhagen in 1847 by Jacob Christian Jacobsen. J.C. Jacobsen was an astute businessman and right from the start banked on high quality for his beer and new styles.

Pampered and cuddled

However, as is often the case in families of headstrong entrepreneurs, there was friction between J.C. and his son Carl. Carl snubbed his father and set up his own brewery, the Ny (New) Carlsberg, as a result of which his father renamed his brewery Gamle Carlsberg (Old Carlsberg). Early on, the two Carlsberg breweries proved their technological and organisational superiority and began to dominate the Danish beer market. The government at the time showed great interest in the development of the brewing industry and the rapid growth of the market leader, Carlsberg. It was not concerned with encouraging competition, though, only on preserving the steady stream of beer taxes. Small wonder there was no resistance from the government when, in 1895, Carlsberg and Tuborg established a cartel, which was expanded into a trust system with shared profits in 1903. By this stage, the two Carlsberg breweries had been reunited again under the control of one Foundation. Being the larger company with lower unit costs in the trust system, Carlsberg was to benefit most from the shared profits and the tempering of the winds of competition.

In the following decades Carlsberg enjoyed optimal greenhouse conditions for growth. It became a local hero, whose international activities revolved around direct beer exports and getting involved in sales and brewing joint ventures abroad. Blessed with an unchallenged domestic profit pool and calmly steered by the Foundation, Carlsberg prospered. The management was professional, Danish, not restricted to family, but chosen on merit. Unlike many beer cartels in other countries, the Danish club held firm for a long time. As a matter of fact, it only came to an end when Carlsberg merged with Tuborg in 1970. With everything quiet on the home front – the cartel plus restrictions on competition took care of that – Carlsberg and Tuborg could devote their attention to foreign markets. Shrewdly, they avoided setting up shop in the same markets, so that they could carve up the world between themselves.

The big leap forward

Carlsberg's motto, *Laboremus pro patria* (Let us work for our country), chiselled in stone on the famous Elephant gate at Ny Carlsberg Vej, should actually have read: 'do-ut-des', I give so that you will give. The Fatherland, at least, got the message, and in 1970 showed gratitude when it allowed Carlsberg to merge with Tuborg to become United Breweries. It should be noted that such a deal would not meet with regulatory approval today. In all likelihood it was the Danish tax man, swooning at the prospect of increased excise revenues, who pushed the merger through. Ultimately, United Breweries became a quasi-monopoly in its domestic market, on top of being the sole purveyor of Danish beer in foreign markets. Although in actual fact the whole of the Danish beer profit pool was controlled by Carlsberg, management still thought it necessary to keep up appearances of there being two companies, and for several years an artificial division was maintained. The Tuborg site in Hellerup was kept open and United Breweries' CEO Svanholm split his time commuting between his desks in Hellerup and Copenhagen.[3] When no opposition to the new monopolist was eventually forthcoming, the window-dressing was abandoned and United Breweries was renamed Carlsberg, full stop. Production moved from the Hellerup site to Carlsberg's plant in Federicia and the Tuborg property was put on the market.

The business card strategy

Bolstered by a steady stream of dependable profits, Carlsberg continued to raise its profile abroad. In the early days of the internationalisation of the brewing industry, foreign forays were often haphazard. Whoever dropped in on a particular brewer's headquarters and left their business card stood a good chance of becoming an importer or a licensee. It would not have been much different in Carlsberg's case.[4] In this way a number of markets were conquered by accident or by chance, like Malawi in 1968. Others were opportunistic occasions; somebody came round the corner with a bargain offer that seemed too good to refuse. Systematic search, or even the much-touted 'buy in and develop' tactics, did not figure on the agenda. Apart from anything else, back then Carlsberg lacked the resources (i.e. personnel) to analyse, detect and attack new markets. An export division worthy of the name did not exist, and Carlsberg's sales organisation was fragmented. This strange state-of-affairs – the decentralisation of decision-making and control – has been a prominent feature of Carlsberg and, for better or for worse, probably lives on in some areas today.

In spite of this, Carlsberg has displayed a penchant throughout its history for implementing technological and scientific developments in brewing. In an industry set on growth, this was a Unique Selling Proposition that served Carlsberg well. Anyone with a production or quality problem was welcome to seek advice from Carlsberg, Tuborg or the affiliate, Danbrew. Embracing the role of a technology partner, Carlsberg found its calling and entered into the first phase of larger-scale international expansion. This approach bears striking similarities to Löwenbräu's in the 1980s. Theirs were both fine and well-defined brands, very nice beers and technically, unquestionably, extremely sophisticated. Do many people still remember Löwenbräu? No? Well, it seems this approach did not present a sustainable growth pattern.

Lateral diversification

By the mid-1990s, Carlsberg had reached an impasse. From a small regional brewer it had managed to turn itself into a Nordic Power.[5] But, among its peers, the now seventh-ranking brewer in the world had the poorest margins. All the while big European brewers like Heineken and Interbrew embarked on a massive shopping spree, snapping up breweries left, right and centre, Carlsberg's empire remained a patchwork. Scattered around the Danish beer business you would have found an assortment of holdings with little business logic to connect them: Royal Scandinavia, 'a top of the line houseware operation', wine importers, soft drink distribution, supermarkets.[6] While Carlsberg believed it had invested its profits in highly attractive markets, the numbers proved the opposite, and margins were deteriorating. Actually, Carlsberg completely missed the first round of globalisation in the beer industry and did not jump boldly onto the opportunities which offered themselves.[7] Still, a variety of export markets were dealt with, while licensed production and minority interests in breweries were becoming the standard. But Carlsberg did not have much of a say in its co-operative ventures. Foreign returns remained few and far between and often the sign on a number was not the right one. Even when Carlsberg was the majority stakeholder in a foreign venture, it should have realised on closer scrutiny that these businesses were either mistakes or badly run. When it came to managing large local units Carlsberg appeared out of its depth. The local CEOs basically did what they thought was right, often at the expense of the profitability of the parent Carlsberg, as the Danish failed to keep them on a short leash.

The Danish star in the German rough

Poor local management capability was certainly the problem in the largest beer market in Europe before the fall of the Iron Curtain, namely Germany. Both Carlsberg and Tuborg had signed licensing agreements with the then well-known brewers Deutsche Brauholding/ Bavaria St Pauli in Hamburg and the Hannen Brauerei in Mönchengladbach. In Hamburg the licence languished and did so for a long time, while Hannen was acquired quickly to allow Carlsberg to expand into this exciting market. That was the theory. The business was headed by local managers as Carlsberg could only provide technical staff and number-crunchers, but no marketing and sales people who could operate and shape distant markets, let alone leaders who were genuine CEO material. Hence Carlsberg remained dependent on local talent, who were given free rein, not out of conviction but due to a lack of vision.

Carlsberg wasn't bothered about developing this resource and didn't even feel the need to do so. Therefore, as the Carlsberg brand rose to become a major seller at the discount retailer Aldi (did no one spot the discrepancy between the brand's claim – probably the best beer in the world – and its price positioning?) and the local Carlsberg/ Hannen managers, according to estimates, accumulated considerable carry-forward losses, all Copenhagen could do was to watch the tragedy unfold from the sidelines. Having taken pride in volume sales going north, Copenhagen chose to turn a blind eye to profits going south. When the German government introduced the controversial deposit on non-returnable beverage packaging on 1 January 2003 the bubble burst and the party was over. The Hannen brewery was quietly sold to the German cheap beer producer Oettinger in a fire sale the same year. What remained of this venture were the accumulated losses.

Pride and prejudice

Over in the UK it was not an exactly identical story but, nevertheless, Carlsberg delivered similar results. Britain used to be the main export market for Carlsberg. It entered the UK proper in 1974 when it set up its own production. The market's profitability was mainly driven by the on-trade (pubs and bars), and the basis for Carlsberg's on-trade presence was the tied pubs owned by the beer, drinks and property group Grand Metropolitan. In the early 1980s, the British Monopolies & Mergers Commission began to develop a dislike of these arrangements and in 1989 the UK government followed suit by introducing the Beer Orders, which severed the tie between brewers and their pub estates.

Suddenly, the high margins in the on-trade were a thing of the past. Carlsberg had to increase its market share to continue enjoying its share of that market's profits. However, the planned merger of brewers Carlsberg Tetley and Bass in 1996 fell foul of the competition authorities. What is more, Carlsberg UK failed to extract itself from its thankless 'sandwich position'. As a perennial number four player in the market, Carlsberg ended up 'stuck in the middle', in the terminology of Harvard economist Michael E Porter. It was neither big enough to exercise any market power nor small enough to fill a profitable niche.

Site closures and a rapid succession of restructuring programmes were meant to return Carlsberg to profitability. But the local management never succeeded in making the turnaround, not even in 2004, when a powerful competitor brand, Holsten, joined Carlsberg UK's portfolio. Fast forward to 2015, and Carlsberg was still ranked number four brewer in the UK. The importance of the Carlsberg brand had dwindled to such an extent that the supermarket chain Tesco could afford to boot it off its shelves almost completely. The reason given: It did not meet volume targets.[8]

In 1996 Mr Svanholm retired from Carlsberg. Fortunately, his successor, Flemming Lindeløv, acknowledged that Carlsberg needed to get out of its 'Nordic Trap'. Quickly, non-core ventures were sold and beer became the core business. But Mr Lindeløv's acquisitions machinery often jammed. He only succeeded in clinching minor deals because his daring bid for Whitbread Brewing and Bass Brewers in 2000 was bettered by Interbrew.[9] Not least due to Carlsberg's rigid shareholder structure, the takeover of French brewer Kronenbourg, which was owned by

Danone, in the same year, came to nothing. Danone wanted to be paid in cash and in Carlsberg shares. The Foundation's charter, which stipulated that it must hold the majority of the voting rights and the majority of the share capital in Carlsberg A/S, proved a major obstacle. This time, rather than protecting Carlsberg against hostile takeovers, it acted as a brake on an acquisition. Whoever wanted to globalise Carlsberg had to solve this problem, or at least come up with a work-around plan.

The window of opportunity

At the turn of the 21st century, Mr Lindeløv pulled off a real feat – a U-turn in a cul-de-sac – which is one way to view the tie-up between Carlsberg A/S and Orkla ASA in 2000, which led to the founding of Carlsberg Breweries, the joint venture vehicle for both their beverage interests. Remarkably, the new venture shook up Carlsberg's world. Firstly, at long last Carlsberg started registering real growth and had even found a partner, despite the restrictions imposed by the Foundation's charter. Secondly, Carlsberg's monopoly suddenly extended to the whole of northern Europe. Thirdly, the brewer was opening itself up to a new management structure. Fourthly, it entered – or was dragged into – the Russian market.

How come? Like Carlsberg, the Norwegian Orkla was a Nordic stock market heavyweight, albeit with a much more aggressive and successful mergers and acquisitions track record than the somewhat sluggish Carlsberg A/S. Orkla's investment portfolio was one of the largest in Norway. Dating back to the 17th century with roots in the mining industry, Orkla had been expanding into the metal processing and chemical industries, complemented by a strong branded consumer goods segment in foods and media.[10] Merging with Nora Industrier in 1991, the group became the largest beverage producer in Norway (Ringnes Group). Orkla bulked up, especially internationally, when it acquired the Swedish food companies Procordia and Abba Seafood from Volvo in 1995. Part of the package was made up of Sweden's major brewer, Pripps. Pripps and Ringnes were subsequently merged to become Pripps Ringnes AB, which also had a stake in Finland's Hartwall and Baltic Beverages Holding (BBH), the market leader in Finland, the Baltics and St Petersburg/Russia.[11] The combined group's market position was impressive and the anti-trust watchdogs grew restless. In due course, though, approval was granted, on the condition that Pripps Ringnes disposed of Hansa Bryggeri, Norway's number two brewer.[12]

A Viking white knight

Unbeknown to many, Orkla had managed to achieve monopoly positions in Norway and Sweden, comparable to Carlsberg's position in the (much smaller) Danish beer market. But unlike Carlsberg, Orkla's executives not only saw that the brewing industry was consolidating and globalising quickly, they also wanted to be part of it, realising that being the market leader in the Nordic markets was no guarantee of a big share of the global beer profit pool. So Orkla set out to find itself an experienced partner and Carlsberg seemed like a good choice.

South of the Skagerrak (the strait between Norway and Sweden), frustration levels were rising, causing Carlsberg to embark on a frantic search for a partner, especially when the failed Kronenbourg deal drove home the message that, in order to play Beer Monopoly, Carlsberg needed funds or the option to take a partner on board. The work-around plan was born: Carlsberg was to become a two-tier holding.

On 31 May 2000 Orkla and Carlsberg announced the formation of Carlsberg Breweries, 'one of the world's largest beer companies' to be headquartered in Copenhagen.[13] The founders would contribute the lion's share of their respective beverage portfolios to Carlsberg Breweries, which thus became 'the market leader in the Nordic countries and the leading brewery company in the rapidly growing market in Russia, the Baltic States and Ukraine and in parts of Asia'.[14]

Initially, it seemed as if the Norwegians were to determine the group's strategic direction for the next 15 years. After all, Orkla's dowry included its 50 percent stake in the rapidly expanding BBH. Observers say that Carlsberg's swerve towards Russia, originally, was accidental. Only years later did Carlsberg declare it the result of a deliberate strategy change because it needed a justification for its stubborn pursuit of the UK brewer Scottish & Newcastle (taken over by Carlsberg in 2008), its 50 percent partner in BBH.

The failure of the cultural revolution

The establishing of Carlsberg Breweries marked a quantum leap for Carlsberg in many respects. The joint venture had a turnover of about $5 billion, an operating profit of nearly $300 million and employed 27,000 people. Carlsberg A/S controlled 60 percent of the shares, Orkla 40 percent. This split was mirrored by the distribution of seats in the executive management and the board of directors. However, the rumour mill posed this question: Would this allow Carlsberg Breweries to continue to be a truly Danish company, considering the Norwegians' ego and resolve?

Not only did the Norwegian and Swedish investors in Orkla have a more successful international track record than the Danish but, even before pooling their beverage interests with Carlsberg's, Orkla generated more than half its revenues abroad. Besides, Orkla's targets as concerns business dynamics, efficiency and results appeared to be significantly higher than Carlsberg's. This alone should have persuaded Carlsberg to realign its management culture. But did Carlsberg seize the opportunity? Circumstantial evidence suggests they did not. When entering into the venture with Carlsberg, Orkla's idea was to steadily raise margins and profits at Carlsberg Breweries and to clinch more deals.[15] There were no indications that Orkla would want to exit the joint venture a few years later. It soon became an open secret that the partners did not get on well, either culturally or strategically. In 2004 Carlsberg acquired Orkla's 40 percent stake at a premium for $3.3 billion and became the sole owner of Carlsberg Breweries.

Conscious uncoupling

Although, in financial terms, the exit paid off handsomely for Orkla, this sale would not necessarily have been Orkla's preferred option from the start. Within a few years, nearly all of the Norwegians and Swedes had departed from Carlsberg's top management. Was it the Danes' refusal to work with non-Danes on an equal basis? One thing is certain: The Danes were again home alone, which was just as they liked it best. But as the floodwaters of recession rose a decade later, Carlsberg was finally forced to internationalise its management, and in 2015 they appointed a Dutchman as CEO.

With Orkla's departure, Carlsberg not only missed the chance to develop a different management culture, it also proved to the world that it could not grow by taking on a partner. Theoretically, the intermediary holding company, Carlsberg Breweries, was an excellent vehicle. In practice, however, achieving a cultural consensus with different partners remains an elusive goal. Carlsberg rides alone and, so far, Carlsberg has refrained from repeating the experiment. It would rather take money from the banks than enter into another marriage.

The manic era

In 2001 Mr Lindeløv was succeeded by the Carlsberg veteran Nils Andersen as CEO. The financial controllers took over in Copenhagen and were tasked with pruning costs. To put it another way, the easy times were over.

In the early Noughties, Russia and Ukraine became Carlsberg's El Dorado, which raised Carlsberg's dependence on these markets disproportionately. By 2009, eastern Europe contributed over 50 percent to Carlsberg's profits, hence Mr Hansmaennel's joke at the time that Carlsberg had turned itself into a Russian brewer with European subsidiaries. The gains from eastern Europe were not just in terms of cash flow. Carlsberg had shown that it could 'do' acquisitions and subsequently achieve organic growth and profit increases, and so were an accolade for Carlsberg's management and its capabilities. It was also proof that Carlsberg had become a global player. However, the reliance on eastern Europe put Carlsberg in a quandary: good news from the east had to keep coming. Carlsberg's management developed a keen ear, but its hypersensitivity gradually turned into an obsession.

Driving performance excellence

One corollary of Carlsberg's new found riches in eastern Europe was that its subsidiaries in western and northern Europe were downgraded to mere suppliers of cash flow, and so did not receive much investment in brands, markets and production. Instead, they witnessed asset stripping, the sale of real estate, and the closure of production sites. A series of Excellence Programmes was launched. For business consultants this would have been the dawn of a golden era. To outsiders, it must have seemed as if the Carlsberg organisation had no skills to cope with the modern times. In rapid succession modules such as COMEX (Commercial Excellence), PRODEX (Production Excellence), LOGEX (Logistics Excellence) and AdmEx (Administration Excellence) were rolled out. These programmes were declared 'Must-Win-Battles' to emphasise that they were not just run-of-the-mill cost-cutting exercises.[16]

At the subsidiaries, people frequently rubbed their eyes in disbelief as yet another youngster was put in charge without any idea what the beer business was about. Criticism, even constructive criticism, was not welcome. Local units were learning quickly that it was best not to be the noisiest boy in the classroom, but to keep their heads down. In spite of all this, efficiencies increased. Whether they were sustainable in the long run was another issue. As far as top-line growth was concerned, the programmes were a disaster. Brands and markets slipped out of focus as the sales strategy became exclusively volume-oriented, and product quality suffered. Nevertheless, Mr Andersen is credited with having laid the foundations for the modern Carlsberg and launched a new global strategy in terms of marketing, corporate culture and production/logistics.[17]

Razing an alpine stronghold …

Although mature beer markets were never really the flavour of the month with analysts due to their slow growth and demographic outlook, Carlsberg in the Noughties decided to expand into these self-same markets through acquisitions. Strangely, it appeared as if the financial controllers were in charge of these deals, given that they were all about buy and break up, immediate synergies and short-term profits. An explanation for this anomaly is that Carlsberg was strapped for funds and the invested cash had to be returned quickly. As to the long-term earnings potential of these markets – it was disdainfully ignored.

The first mature market to receive the Carlsberg makeover was Switzerland. In 2000 Carlsberg bought the Feldschlösschen brewery, which was founded in 1876 and was for a long time Switzerland's major beer company. The way the Swiss saw it, it was an emergency exit; Feldschlösschen's returns were low.[18] No wonder the sales price of $544 million looked like a bargain.[19] Wasting no time, Carlsberg made sure that the investment flowed back promptly and a Danish crew was dispatched to Switzerland to trim Feldschlösschen to profitability. The Swiss suffered a culture shock and management took flight.

… and the marshes of northern Germany

Next Carlsberg reentered Germany, then the world's 4th largest beer market. Carlsberg Breweries acquired Germany's Holsten Group for a total consideration of $1.34 billion. The purpose of this re-entry shortly after the Hannen calamity only became apparent when the proceeds from the dismantling of the group were taken into account. The ink on the contract with Holsten was barely dry when Carlsberg sold the König and Licher breweries to the Bitburger Brewery Group, and the Hansa-Heemann Group (water and non-alcoholic beverages) to the Lange family. These disposals netted Carlsberg roughly $800 million.[20] Not included were the so-called peripherals of the Holsten takeover. Further asset stripping and the relocation of Holsten's export and license businesses to Carlsberg ExLid, BBH and Carlsberg UK, might have added up to another several hundred million euros.

Seen in this light, Carlsberg's second entry into the German market was less about expanding the southern borders of its Scandinavian stronghold, as German media suspected; it was primarily meant to compensate Carlsberg for the losses incurred from the previous German venture. Ultimately, the purchase of Holsten more than paid for itself and Carlsberg showed that it could think and act like a private equity company too.

While the Holsten deal may have made financial sense, the subsequent vertical expansion into the German wholesale sector (route-to-market) made no sense whatsoever. The German wholesaler is – apologies for being blunt – a glorified truck driver, not a beer marketer and certainly not the master of its customers' portfolio. The route-to-market is an arena for everyone who wants to do battle over price and terms; there is no exclusivity. In the end, Carlsberg's venture into the German wholesale sector only resulted in a distraction from the brand business and diluted returns. In lieu of a fattening cash cow it got itself a repairs operation.

Carry on regardless

In spite of the various excellence programmes, Carlsberg, it has to be said, managed to maintain an amazing resistance to advice and learning from experience. In Italy, too, Carlsberg had fruitlessly attempted to stabilise its market share by branching out into distribution. This was undoubtedly a costly experience, and one which was now being repeated in Germany.

Unwilling to accept that the route-to-market was country-specific and that there wasn't a one-size-fits-all solution, Carlsberg continued to plough money into these ventures. Perhaps the big bosses were too far away, liaison officers too naive and the local management too power-conscious to admit to mistakes. Whatever the case, Carlsberg revealed a flaw in its governance, which would continue to plague it. Its empire was more of a loose union than an absolute monarchy, and as long as the local barons delivered and executed the excellence programmes carefully, they were free to do as they thought right. There was far too little central control over local markets, brands or marketing, and Copenhagen's insight into the strengths and strategic values of the group's local brands was poor. Carlsberg's corporate marketing and sales team, when compared with its peers, exercised scant control over the local fiefs' decisions, whose goal was short-term profit maximisation.

Fortunately, the rapid rise of the Russian beer market prevented analysts from looking too closely at what was going on elsewhere in Carlsberg's empire. It certainly blinded management in Copenhagen. Once Carlsberg's CEO Andersen left the brewer to become CEO of the Danish shipping company Moeller Maersk and handed over to Jørgen Buhl Rasmussen in 2007, Carlsberg's priorities were crystal clear: BBH!

The obsessive era

Deliberately misquoting Karl Marx, observers concurred that 'a spectre is haunting Copenhagen – the spectre of the philanderer'. Although Carlsberg was free to return to its preferred Danish monoculture after the divorce from Orkla, the Danes were deeply troubled by having to share the management of BBH with their British rivals, the brewer Scottish & Newcastle (S&N), aka the philanderer. As if to spite the Danish, the Finnish part-owners of BBH had sold themselves to S&N in 2002. Relations between Carlsberg and S&N in BBH were not acrimonious or heavily conflict-laden, but this did not prevent Carlsberg from fretting over possible future dissent (other people would call this paranoia), especially when S&N put itself up for sale and potential buyers began to queue outside its door: InBev, Anheuser-Busch, Heineken, and SABMiller. Amateur psychology aside, the acquisition of the outstanding 50 percent stake in BBH, and the subsequent separation from the current joint venture partner, suddenly took precedence for Carlsberg's management. Sharing the spoils in BBH with yet another competitor? This must not be allowed to happen at any price.

Creating the world's fastest-growing brewer

What followed is the most expensive deal ever clinched by a Danish stock market-listed company. In late 2007, Carlsberg and Heineken set up Sunrise Acquisitions[21], their vehicle to jointly take over S&N for what can only be described as an inflated price. Hats off to S&N. The Brits had forced Carlsberg and Heineken to put $15.4 billion on the table, or 15 times S&N's profits (EBITDA) according to the bank Nomura. Carlsberg's share in the transaction was 56 percent. The high valuation was primarily driven by the growth prospects in the Baltics, the Ukraine and Russia. Carlsberg assumed that BBH would raise volume sales annually by 14 percent to reach 69 million hl beer in 2010. Forecasted EBITDA (in 2010) was €1.25 billion

($1.8 billion).[22] Alas, Carlsberg got its timing wrong and the takeover company should have better been called Sunset Acquisitions because the deal was sealed on 25 January 2008, the year that saw the financial crisis shake global markets and the Russian economy nosedive. Carlsberg's covenants with the banks were at risk. This was the finest hour of all finance honchos in the Carlsberg Group. Resolutely, they squeezed every cent in profit and cash flow out of the subsidiaries. When Carlsberg showed it was capable of meeting the conditions of the covenants, the banks heaved a sigh of relief and the deal went through.

Actually, the S&N deal would not have been possible without generating additional equity. The Foundation's charter was rewritten in 2008 so that it continued to control 51 percent of the voting rights, but its share of capital was diluted to 30 percent.[23]

The change in the Foundation's charter had brought flexibility, yet room for future manoeuvres was becoming increasingly smaller. With almost clairvoyant lucidity, in January 2008 the Swiss newspaper *Neue Zürcher Zeitung* ran a story under the following headline: 'Carlsberg's cocky leadership'.[24] Carlsberg A/S proudly talked about, in the invitation to its Annual General Meeting in 2008, 'Creation of the World's Fastest Growing Global Brewer'. In the investor presentation the core message of CEO Jørgen Buhl Rasmussen and CFO Jørn Paul Jensen was: Full control of our destiny! The relief was palpable; the spectre was banished, the nightmares were gone.

Driving excellence – again

Carlsberg's new strategy was entitled 'Transformation of Carlsberg'[25] with the objectives of improving earnings in western Europe, achieving profitable growth in BBH and eastern Europe, building a platform in Asia and developing real estate.

Carlsberg had chosen, and had also decided what it could do without. It waived the markets in the Americas, Africa and Australia. Western and eastern Europe were to grow organically and profitably, and the much-trumpeted excellence programmes would take care of the rest. At the end, there was the admission, though, that its financial corset was a bit tight. As to 'developing real estate', this could only mean that cash was king. Flogging its hidden assets was already part of its long-term financing.

However, the promises of victory were houses built on sand. 'Achieving European Leadership' suggested that Carlsberg would soon be the market leader in Europe. In 2008 Heineken was the undisputed King of Beer in Europe, but of course not for long (if Carlsberg's plans had anything to do with it). In eastern Europe, the dynamically growing market, Carlsberg was better positioned than its peers. Therefore, in Carlsberg's view, 'European Leadership' was only a matter of time and statistical extrapolation. Fully aware that Russia was an emerging market, which had seen its ups and downs, Carlsberg still preferred to ignore the possibility of a slowdown in eastern Europe, although there were warning signs as early as 2007. This begs the question: Did Carlsberg's leadership really understand how its risk profile had changed? The cushion of unrealised gains had probably already been consumed or budgeted for; the cash cows in western Europe would find it exceedingly difficult to reach targets; Asia might deliver but only in the distant future. In spite of all that, Carlsberg bet on red: Russia.

Twilight of the gods

Perhaps punch-drunk from celebrating its triumphant takeover of S&N, Carlsberg did not see that the introduction of the accelerated beer tax in Russia in 2008, which had been in the pipeline for some time, would just be a first step by the government to curb beer consumption. In rapid succession the Russian government has since rolled out a strict anti-alcohol campaign, which not only legally defined beer as an alcoholic drink, but increased the duty for beer, applied limitations to beer advertising, banned the sale of beer in kiosks and, in June 2016, restricted the size of beer bottles to no bigger than 1.5 litres (Russians preferred to buy beer in very large plastic bottles). Isn't it ironic that in 2008, when Carlsberg snapped up S&N, Russia's beer market peaked at 120 million hl? Since then it contracted to 69 million hl in 2015. The beer market has not quite halved, but that is a loss of 40 percent and there are no indications that the decline will bottom out any time soon.

Currently, breweries in Russia are working at half capacity and companies are reducing costs by closing plants. In 2015, Carlsberg had to mothball three of its ten breweries across Russia, while sales declined and profits dropped. Compared with its competitors AB-InBev, Heineken and Turkish Efes, Carlsberg steered through the crisis relatively well. Its profits in 2014 were 16.8 billion roubles (€230 million / $317 million), while Heineken posted a loss and the other two scraped by, according to data released released in February 2016.[26] Bearing in mind that it had originally forecasted over €1 billion (see above) in annual profits from Russia, this can be no consolation to Carlsberg.

The clear warnings that the Russian beer market could have passed its peak and that the era of Russia's liberal market economy might draw to a close were already being studiously ignored during the S&N acquisition. Only when Russian beer sales began their steep decline and foreign brewers had to mull over which of their brand new breweries to shut down under the new confiscatory scenario (for lack of a nicer term), did Carlsberg's management and supervisory board in Copenhagen begin to panic. Adding to their woes is China, which has become a major investment, but provides poor results. Northern and western Europe have not received any TLC (i.e. tender loving care) for years, leaving them with an eroded revenue base. And now the crown jewel is turning into costume jewellery; Baltika can no longer deliver as was hoped. And what is delivered is in Russian roubles, a currency worth less by the day.

The meltdown of the power plant

The near-collapse of the Russian beer market for Carlsberg was almost akin to the meltdown of a Russian nuclear power plant. In September 2012, the *Financial Times*' Richard Milne already rated the situation in Russia as having dealt Carlsberg a 'devastating blow'.[27] If Carlsberg's management was nervous, the Foundation must have been frantic. To coin a phrase, its foundations had been shaken. Sustainable profits, no risks, a secure and steady income for the Foundation's purpose, all was about to vanish into thin air. From where the Foundation stood, the accumulation of Russian risk because of Carlsberg's one-sided dependence on its Russian business must have been borderline-folly. None of Carlsberg's multinational competitors had such a pronounced risk profile. Whether he was aware of it or not, Carlsberg's CEO Rasmussen was sitting in an ejector seat right from the start, which was eventually triggered by Mr Putin.

Carlsberg's problems became so overwhelming that in 2015 Mr Rasmussen had to strike his colours and a small revolution was staged. Cees 't Hart, a foreigner, was appointed CEO of Carlsberg. Imagine, Carlsberg, the global player which had never been international in the fullest sense, but in essence had always remained a 'standard-bearer for Danish culture'[28], was to be run by a Dutchman. The retirement of Carlsberg's executive suite was completed when CFO Jensen departed following Mr 't Hart's appointment.

What now? Frankly, things could have been worse. Carlsberg's Russian unit Baltika was the only foreign-controlled market player that had so far managed to come out of the crisis alive. However, is there any guarantee that the situation will not get worse? The soft scenario for the Russian beer market is a further decline in purchasing power; the hard-scenario is the expulsion of foreign investors. As one insider said, the foreign brewers are a far more tempting target than the domestic liquor producers.[29] More than ever, the Russian market is fraught with all kinds of imponderable risks.

The battle for the future

After the baton was passed to him, Mr 't Hart immediately and skilfully sounded a note of warning. Announcing Carlsberg's half year results on 19 August 2015, he slipped the public and shareholders the hint of a profit warning ('revised 2015 earnings expectation') and had already identified the culprits. It was the bad weather (once again), the stagnation in western European markets, and the well-known difficulties in eastern Europe. Well-hidden was the admission that Carlsberg was unable to realise its cost reduction potentials. In Carlsberg's Annual Report 2015[30] the hint was made explicit. The 'revised 2015 earnings expectations' was merely a 'profit warning' in disguise. The old management had departed, the problems remained.

Together with his top-60 leadership team Mr 't Hart set to work. Basically, the new Carlsberg management was trying to give the clear impression that it had the strategies and concepts needed to turn Carlsberg around. The magic phrase was SAIL '22, its strategy up until 2022, and it rested on 'Funding the Journey'. Both documents, in their final versions, were presented to investors in March 2016. Probably in an effort to calm the markets, most of the information was leaked in advance. The Annual Report 2015, published on 24 February 2016, announced the strategy officially. On 16 March 2016 Cees 't Hart and

Chris Warmoth finally explained SAIL '22 and 'Funding the Journey' to analysts in a conference call.

The word count was impressive, although content and claim were somewhat thin. As was to be expected, markets and analysts were underwhelmed.[31] The lofty slogans and their constant repetition could not conceal the fact that the top-60 team had not come up with anything new. Many would have preferred to hear details of a genuine turnaround at Carlsberg, instead of the proposed evolution. Too much old wine in new bottles, really.

Sail away, dream your dreams

The strategy paper's biggest surprise was the statement that Carlsberg would continue to sell beer because it was an interesting consumer category. However, they were not alone in having had this idea, Jorge Paulo Lemann, one of the major shareholders of AB-InBev, being another one. Forbes magazine considers him one of the wealthiest men in the world, ranked 19th on its Rich List (29 May 2016) with an estimated fortune of $31.4 billion – and rising. The source of his wealth? Beer, self-made.[32]

Readers of SAIL '22 were in for another surprise when they learnt Carlsberg's reasons for its current malaise and its proposed remedies. Carlsberg seemed to have been very badly organised. In his crew, Mr 't Hart missed the 'winning culture', the 'focus on delivery and performance'.[33] Carlsberg's teams lacked the will to go the extra mile. As of now, employees' dedication to their job was on the agenda and it would be measured. 'Accountability for delivering results' based on 'rigorous tracking mechanisms' would put people on track. In order for employees to find the right track, a 'tight alignment between management incentive plan and financial objectives' would be provided.[34] Who would have thought? Has not the 'winning culture' been high on Carlsberg's agenda since 2000 when Mr Andersen threw Carlsberg into those 'Must-Win-Battles'? Anyone familiar with the previous Carlsberg incentive schemes and the target agreements for the various management levels will know that Carlsberg has long cracked the whip. As to the key term 'accountability', the true representation of the company's assets, financial position and performance – maybe it would help if Carlsberg were to describe its circumstances in some countries more accurately and would stop sugar coating?[35]

Carlsberg's metric universe

Contrary to its claims, Carlsberg is the major shareholder (44 percent) in Portugal's number one brewer Unicer but it is not number one brewer in the market; Carlsberg Germany operates two breweries in northern Germany, but is not the number two brewer in the market – it ranks eleventh.[36] Even before dismantling the Holsten-Brauerei AG Carlsberg did not have a market share of 16 percent. And arbitrarily reducing the geographical market area to 'northern Germany', whatever that is, does not make the statistics truthful. In China there is no one except Carlsberg who would call Carlsberg the number one brewer. The addendum 'number one in western China' adds little clarification. To claim a 55 percent market share amounts to a gross disrespect for the maths.

What becomes glaringly obvious is that Carlsberg lacks excellence in marketing execution. In most of its core markets in western Europe, Carlsberg has been losing market share to its competitors. Nevertheless, in its half year results 2015, Carlsberg's management almost raved about its sales performance. When comparing market share data for 2005 and 2015, figures tell a different story.[37] In Germany, Europe's largest market, Carlsberg has fared miserably. What remained of the acquired 7.9 million hl beer business (market share: 8.3 percent) in 2004, was 2.6 million hl (market share: 3.1 percent) in 2015. In Denmark and in Sweden, likewise, market shares had to be relinquished. In Italy, Poland and the UK Carlsberg is still unfavourably positioned as number three or four brewer. These markets are not sustainably profitable, whether we talk about 2015 or 2005, despite the many restructurings, staff reductions and site closures in the decade under review.

Moreover, the market share metric does not fully reflect economic reality. 'Market share' refers to volumes sold, not turnover. In Carlsberg's case, the large-scale pricing down of many of its brands and the increased frequency of price promotions have probably hurt Carlsberg's share of the beer profit pool far more than the decline in market share would indicate. Beer production in Europe, excluding Russia and Ukraine, has dropped 8 percent since 2005, or the equivalent of Spain going dry. A marker of good performance is management's ability to increase market share in a declining market. But to go down with the market is a poor show.

A survival plan in disguise

As some have pointed out, SAIL ’22 is not a strategy, it is a survival plan. Those analysts who were deeply dissatisfied with this unimaginative strategy paper may like to consider the possibility that Mr ’t Hart had been hogtied. Ultimately, the whole SAIL ’22 brochure is a long-winded way of saying ‘keep it up’ and ‘no experiments, please’. It is yet another combing through the same organisation to mobilise the last resources that might have escaped the previous cull.

And the market? It is hard to believe that a 120 million hl beer producer like Carlsberg will find salvation in diversifying into craft brewing (SAIL ’22 says it will look at craft). Craft beer is the realm of personality brewers, who can put a face to their beers. Forging alliances with craft brewers requires personalities on Carlsberg’s side with a long shelf life and social skills. In the past, this was not Carlsberg’s style or forte. This is not to rule out corporations from tapping into the craft beer market. AB-InBev is doing just that, buying up craft brewers in a number of different markets around the world. As AB-InBev’s acquisitions show, craft is a buy-and-build business. Since Carlsberg seems to lack the funds to buy at the heady prices successful craft brewers can demand these days, it remains a mystery how Carlsberg is going to manage to turn craft beer into a significant and sizeable business.

Discovering the magic of big cities

The other strategy change that raised a few eyebrows for its banality or obviousness is Carlsberg's decision to make a stronger push into the world's big cities. It sounds a bit odd that in the past Carlsberg should have ignored these markets. Bizarrely, Carlsberg will not try and conquer metropolises in the Americas, as Messrs 't Hart und Warmoth confessed.[38] So which cities are they targeting? Shanghai? Sofia?

Carlsberg's so-called new strategy notwithstanding, are there any other options? There must be. Carlsberg may be the third largest global brewer in terms of total volumes sold, but down on the streets it has not made it into the elite class of market leaders due to its focus and shareholder restrictions. The rules of the game were redrafted by AB-InBev and SABMiller. It may be cruel, but Carlsberg is an oddity in the league it is in. Why not change the league and resize the business? Why not focus on certain markets and pull out from those that cause stress, thus taking complexity out of structure? Naturally, this would mean selling parts that do not deliver and probably never will.

If Carlsberg were to grow through acquisitions within the narrow boundaries of its existing financing, would that make sense? Yet, what is there left to buy? There are no obvious opportunities to buy up complete streets in the Beer Monopoly, as Mr Hansmaennel has shown. Moreover, Carlsberg's chairman has already let it be known that Carlsberg does not have the funds at the moment to finance any acquisitions, although this may not be a bad thing. In the past, Carlsberg has spread itself too thinly in a large number of small deals. Apart from in the Nordic countries, where thanks to Orkla it obtained market leadership, Carlsberg mostly did in-country deals (see China). It was, basically, expansion at random, a grasping at opportunities, but Carlsberg did not create any opportunities itself. Remember, it merged with Tuborg because there was outside pressure; it founded Carlsberg Breweries because Orkla sought to add value to its beverage business; and it bought S&N in an act of passive self-defence because it was afraid of having to work with an unpredictable new partner.

Carlsberg's *mappa mundi*

Looking at the Carlsberg globe, it appears as if the Copernican Revolution never happened. It mainly covers Eurasia and is a flat disk. Dimly, in the south, there was a landmass – or is it an island – called Malawi. But the business was divested in 2016 to France's Castel as Carlsberg pulled out of Africa altogether. In Carlsberg's world, the Americas do not even exist. Today, Carlsberg's strongholds are the same as they were 15 years ago: the Nordic countries. There it enjoys a near-unchallenged position, protected from imports and cheap beers alike, thanks to high alcohol or consumer taxes. The rest may impress, like Vietnam, Switzerland, France and Russia, but recent years have shown that these positions are vulnerable to attacks from the branded competition, price undercutting and the government.

Will China be different? Given that beer consumption in China has declined since 2014 and massively so, Carlsberg could be in for another calamitous experience.

We should not forget that the Chinese market is wide open to imports, especially cheap beer from Germany. In the long run China will not only be the largest beer market in the world, but may also be one of the cheapest. It is tough going, especially in western China – Carlsberg's core market – where the current economic slowdown has hit hard.

This leaves us with the eternal hopeful, India, a federation of 29 states, each with its own tax system, interstate tariffs and different legislations regarding the production and marketing of alcohol. Despite annual consumption growth, the market has remained small. India's beer production was 20.5 million hl in 2015, slightly less than the Netherlands'. Profits on a per hl basis are among the lowest worldwide. Besides, Carlsberg is not even the major brewer here. Heineken, through United Breweries, leads the market, followed by SABMiller's unit. When quizzed about Heineken's future in India, their CEO Jean-François van Boxmeer reportedly said: 'Our investment in India … is for my successor's successor.' While doing business in India can be interesting, sometimes even exciting, there are serious doubts that India can ever become a dazzling growth story for Carlsberg. In summing up, one could say that Carlsberg is in all the wrong markets today.[39]

Dancing with the Russian bear

Peering through Carlsberg's corporate obfuscation and fibbing, one can see that in the future Carlsberg's earnings will hinge on two factors beyond its control: the benevolence of the Russian president and the Russian *nomenklatura*, and the demographic development and per capita consumption in western Europe.

It could be argued that all these difficulties are the consequence of Carlsberg being a truly Danish company. The brewer could not help but embark on a *Sonderweg* because of the demands of the Carlsberg Foundation. It is certain that the Foundation's dominance had far-reaching implications. With the narrow focus on delivery, financial controllers took over and Carlsberg became what it is today – a company controlled by financial controllers. There is nothing wrong with this as long as the number crunchers have strong counterparts in the strategic field. But there were none. Carlsberg's CEOs used to be financial controllers at heart. As such, they were good, but lacking in vision and imagination. Admittedly, there was never room for any other type of leader, considering the agenda of the majority shareholder. Even today, Carlsberg appears over-managed and under-led. This may be a federal democratic approach, but who said that businesses spanning the globe should be run like a green party rainbow coalition?

Focusing on doing things right

Limited in many ways, Carlsberg had to be more focused on doing things right than doing the right things. This became painfully clear in the Beer Monopoly when the Brazilians and South Africans proved that through dealmaking they could create more value (the 1+1=3 formula) and more cash. In Carlsberg's case, if funds were available, Carlsberg invested. The more inexpensive the deal in the end, the more attractive it became. This is why Carlsberg ended up with a high market share in low-yielding western China instead of in the coastal provinces, or with unprofitable wholesale networks in Germany and Italy instead of high-performing brewing and sales operations.

Analysts have politely refrained from spelling it out, but Carlsberg's approach to deal-making has been akin to private equity's: buy low, sell high. Carlsberg is far better at buying into business, creating operational excellence, and splitting up and selling bits and pieces at a high price than at developing markets, brands and creating value. Overall, this is not the AB-InBev way of doing business. Why? Clearly, the ownership structure with all its restrictions and taboos sets narrow limits to Carlsberg's strategic options. Carlsberg's managements have created their *marges de manoeuvre* but that is all.

When comparing Carlsberg to its peers, like SABMiller, the realisation must dawn that Carlsberg has no plan for an endgame; there is no exit strategy. In a sense this is the burden imposed on it by the Carlsberg Foundation. Unlike SABMiller, Carlsberg could never think of selling out and making its shareholders unbelievably rich, because this was never the major shareholder's objective. It is simply not on the agenda of a foundation, which is obliged to provide funds for is clientele in perpetuity.

Whereas Carlsberg's competitors always had a bundle of strategic options to grow their businesses and profits, Carlsberg has been compelled to remain a loner, which is reflected in its strategy – never really a strategy as such, but a tactical plan to carry on and generate cash because this is what the Foundation needs. Given this strategic limitation, Carlsberg could only but fail in trying to keep up with its peers. In today's brewing industry, you either have to be large scale or niche, but you must never be stuck in the middle. Awkwardly enough, this seems to be Carlsberg's preferred position.

The Carlsberg Foundation: Systemic weakness or protective shield?

The Jacobsens transferred their shares in their two breweries, Gamle Carlsberg and Ny Carlsberg, to foundations. In 1902, the foundations combined and ran the breweries as independent economic operations. During Carlsberg's merger with Tuborg to United Breweries (renamed Carlsberg A/S in 1987), the Foundation's charter was revised. It was determined that the Foundation must hold at least 51 percent of the shares and 51 percent of the voting rights. Under these statutes it became nearly impossible to raise capital for acquisitions. Thus, by its nature, the Foundation served as a brake and a safeguard at the same time.

The restrictions on accessing capital work on several levels. Carlsberg A/S cannot raise capital through issuing new shares. According to the earlier charter, the Foundation's stake could be diluted to 51 percent of capital. At this level, however, the Foundation would be compelled to provide capital pro rata in a capital increase. This capital is not available. For the same reason Carlsberg is unable to do a share-swap in the event of an acquisition. This is why the takeover of Danone's brewer Kronenbourg did not come off. The establishing of Carlsberg Breweries together with Orkla in 2000 was a clever work-around, but it came to an end after four years and Carlsberg had to pay off Orkla. Banks and Carlsberg's cash flow provided the funds. In effect, the Orkla deal led to a cash drain; it did not lead to capital creation.

For the acquisition of S&N, the charter was redrafted. The Foundation still had to control 51 percent of the voting rights while the Foundation's minimum share capital was reduced to 30 percent.[40] In 2013 an amendment to the charter gave increased flexibility. The Foundation had to continue to hold at least 51 percent of the voting rights, but the requirement for minimum equity was scrapped.[41] A reduction to zero equity is only a theoretical option. Without any equity, the Foundation would have no rights to dividends, which it needs to fulfil its mission. Even in this scenario, new investors would still not have a say in the company and, furthermore, would have to rely on dividends and the prospect of share price gains determined by factors over which they had no control.

However, thanks to the Foundation's control, Carlsberg A/S will never face a hostile takeover as the statutes prevent any investor from gaining a voting majority. The downside is that shareholders will have to put up with what the Foundation considers a decent return. Relying on predictable annual dividends, the Foundation expects Carlsberg's shares to function like a bond: low risk, high yield, rather like a permanent rental income. Whether Carlsberg's share price goes up is of little relevance to the Foundation. It cannot realise such gains because it cannot sell its shares. This effectively makes Carlsberg's stock *unsuitable for the capital market as, of course, investors expect share price increases; dividends are fine, but shares with an upside potential are more attractive. Ultimately, the Foundation's investment philosophy is a no-no for a capital market-driven investor.*

Apart from these hard financial considerations there are other, soft factors, which restrict Carlsberg in its stratagems. Carlsberg and the Foundation are a Danish crown jewel. That makes Carlsberg sacrosanct in some areas and prohibits a sale or a merger. In the case of the latter, the partner would be unable to redraw the rules, while the restrictions imposed by the Foundation would be unpalatable. It may be a minor point, but relocating the head office or headquarters is out of the question too.

Despite its drawbacks and limitations, everybody at Carlsberg will have absorbed the Foundation's philosophy – from the board of governors to the members of the supervisory board who appoint the CEO. That is why to date Carlsberg's management had to come from the same stable, and a bunker mentality prevailed.

But are we really allowed to interpret the single fact that Carlsberg has recently chosen as its CEO someone who isn't a Dane and cut his teeth in a different industry an indication that the brewer is willing to undergo a cultural sea-change, having finally acknowledged that the tide is turning against it?

THE ROUND-TABLE: A DISCUSSION ON THE STATE OF THE BREWING INDUSTRY

In an effort to describe the globalisation of the brewing industry, we have taken an in-depth look at the four biggest brewers – AB-InBev, SABMiller, Heineken, Carlsberg – and analysed how this process was shaped and who has driven it. But globalisation, like history, knows no end. How will it progress further? In the summer of 2016 we set up a round-table discussion, which was hosted by Michael Schmitt (MS), the publisher of Brauwelt International, who questioned Ina Verstl (IV) and Ernst Faltermeier (EF) in more detail on the past and possible future of the brewing industry that formed the background to our researches for this book.

MS In your book you provide a snapshot on the current state of the Beer Monopoly. There are three major players left, who might continue with empire building. However, economists around the world are already predicting an end to globalisation. Is there something to this argument?

IV As far as the brewing industry is concerned, the large movement of 'buy and build', the creation of empires, has pretty much run its course, simply because there is nothing much meaningful left to buy. I also believe that the globalisation of the brewing industry, the buying into markets, was seen as an opportunity specifically to pre-empt the counter-movement we are witnessing now: protectionism. As the big brewers have long established a presence in each of the key markets where there is money to be made, I don't think that the anti-globalisation trend will upset their businesses much.

EF In my view, consumers have not seen globalisation as a threat or that it has deprived them of anything, certainly when it comes to beers on offer. What we need to acknowledge instead is that through globalisation the big brewers have managed to tap into large profit pools. Could it be that the lucrative buy and build circus has finally attracted the attention of those on federal or local levels, who now want to have some of those spoils for themselves?

MS You have described globalisation as a 'route to empire', to establish the largest realm in the world of beer. Has AB-InBev reached its final position?

IV Before that can be answered, we should first reflect on the strategies brewers adopted to play Beer Monopoly. Have they approached globalisation with an endgame in mind, in terms of Cicero's 'respice finem'? AB-InBev set themselves the goal early on to become number one. For SABMiller it was also clear relatively soon thereafter that by reaching the number two position they could be taken over by the number one at some point. In this sense, SABMiller's strategy allowed them to seek a profitable exit should events turn in this direction.

EF For Heineken and Carlsberg, it meant retaining control of their companies. Both have exhausted all of their available options because they knew that in the endgame scenario they would move up to the next step on the ladder. As they show, you could even play Beer Monopoly strategically for second or third place.

MS Is this situation kind of permanent now for the market leaders or is a shift in the ranking still possible?

IV In the global brewers' ranking, the gap between the number one, two and three player is quite substantial. Nonetheless, in the coming years, Carlsberg, Molson Coors and the Chinese brewing company CR Beer could be battling for third place. There is the chance that the other two could overtake Carlsberg. However, this will not have any material effect on the 'buy and build' tactic.

EF Merging with SABMiller, AB-InBev has attained an enviable position. They are now the second most valuable food conglomerate in the world in terms of stock market capitalisation. And from the perspective of market share, I'm almost tempted to say that they have achieved their goal. But we all know that this is not the end of the story. In our comparison, we have focused exclusively on those in the top four positions, leaving out those that occupy a lower ranking. However, there are powerful groups among the followers up, who may continue to develop and emerge in various constellations. But not everyone is striving for a high value on the stock market. Some brewers may prefer to dominate their markets; to secure market share, profits and dividends over the long term. If necessary, they may embark on 'buy and build'.

Monopolies and competition

MS What is your opinion: do brewers have monopolies? You have often referred to market dominance, or that, ideally, it is simply best to be number one.

IV Naturally, the brewing industry is familiar with classic monopolies where there is only one player. However, as anti-trust watchdogs will tell you, markets already suffer from monopolistic conditions if the largest competitor commands a market share of more than 30 percent (UK) or more than 50 percent (USA). But this terminology doesn't really get us far in Beer Monopoly. As craft beer has shown, having the deepest and widest moat around your castle is useless if consumers are given a choice and they go for it. In that case, moats offer no protection and will be overcome.

MS You describe four very different companies in your book, which also pursued four equally different strategies. To what extent have these strategies played a role in determining success and failure?

IV To put it in a nutshell, AB-InBev followed a finance-led growth strategy. By contrast, growth at SABMiller was dictated by shareholder alignment; that is, the focus was always on keeping all principal shareholders on board and convincing them to support the long-term strategy. Heineken has been owned and run by the same family. It has always been of prime importance to the family that they retain control, while Carlsberg had to generate profits to sustain the Carlsberg Foundation. This has had a strong influence on their dealmaking strategies. Who could they afford to buy? Which relationships could they forge and who would be their chosen partners? In my opinion, these structures significantly determined their 'buy and build' activities.

EF If the question is about success or failure, it must be answered in terms of whether they have achieved the goals they set for themselves. There is no such thing as an absolute measure of success. It's interesting to see that Carlsberg has adopted a new strategy in 2016, called SAIL '22 that's quite different from the strategy the company embraced in 2008. Back then the goal was to become the fastest growing global brewer with number one positions both in western Europe and Eurasia. As it turned out, this strategy failed for the most part. The company was forced to restructure and scale back in order to regain control. Carlsberg's risk profile took the brewer past the limits it could safely manage.

IV In this respect, Heineken has fared much better. The company only had limited means to clinch deals and it chose its takeover targets well. As fair competition rules out monopolies, Heineken is in a privileged position now as global number two. It is essential to have at least one other challenger in the market for competition to function. On the global level, Heineken is the only serious competitor for AB-InBev, despite the fact that AB-InBev has many different competitors in individual markets. Heineken has obviously plotted its moves carefully as evidenced by the company's performance on the stock market. What's more, unlike Carlsberg, Heineken did not have to adopt a new strategy. Heineken can simply continue with 'buy and build' or 'build and brew'.

MS Wouldn't you say that in globalisation the finance-led AB-InBev already enjoyed a structural advantage, in that they managed to access the resources of the financial markets more easily than the others?

IV With each takeover, AB-InBev has generated enough profit to finance its next acquisition. And because the Brazilians' goal has always been to be number one, they have perfected their method. AB-InBev got the jump on its competitors by understanding early on that the key to globalisation is dealmaking and empire building. For this reason, its investors have been more than willing to provide support.

EF Heineken's family ownership and Carlsberg's foundation model come with an entire list of restrictions, especially in so far as raising money on the capital markets to finance acquisitions or adding new groups of primary shareholders is concerned. They are slower to react and show a tendency to make smaller, less expensive deals. Given these restrictions, it is particularly challenging for Heineken and Carlsberg to clinch very big deals. In essence, this has never been the case for AB-InBev and SABMiller. They have always been able to finance large and expensive deals, none of which were classified as bad buys, at least not on a scale that would have jeopardised their companies. Many thought, "My God, look how much money is changing hands. It is far too expensive!" But as it turned out, it was never too much to bring the whole edifice down.

MS Heineken and Carlsberg are now ranked second and third. Do their different models as family-owned and foundation-owned brewers provide them with some sort of protection against takeovers?

EF Absolutely. Their models act like a poison pill for every potential buyer. Perhaps this is also the reason why the two did not feature as potential objects of desire in any takeover scenarios. There were far easier targets for investors. One should not forget that even though both companies are stock market-listed and have external shareholders, they function differently.

Who are the losers?

MS Are there also losers in the economic Darwinism that is the Beer Monopoly?

IV Strictly speaking, there has only been one loser so far, and that is Foster's. After receiving a near-fatal battering during the first wave of globalisation in the 1980s, the company adopted the strategy of becoming a leader in the global wine market. This attempt also met with failure because the globalisation of wine does not bear much resemblance to that of beer. When big holes opened up in their wine business, shareholders pulled the plug and had the beer unit sold to SABMiller. If Foster's had not made the fateful decision to move into wine, a decision which was supported by the shareholders at the time, it is possible that Foster's might still be around today as an independent company.

MS If a company is taken over, does this brand the company as a loser?

EF Actually, the only loser would be a company that has been driven so far into a corner that it can only save itself through a fire sale. To my knowledge we have not seen anything of the kind yet. All shareholders with stakes in companies which were taken over seemed to have been very pleased with the generous proceeds from the sale. Likewise those who ended up as part of a larger group …

IV … think of Miller with SABMiller

EF … are faring much better than they would have on their own.

IV The Anheuser-Busch takeover was touted as hostile. But despite the rhetoric, it was the shareholders who gave it the thumbs up. The reason: InBev's $53 billion offer was simply too good to pass up. If anyone, it is the Busch family, who had steered the brewery for generations, who could be construed as the losers in this deal. However, since the Buschs no longer had a majority stake in the company, others were allowed to determine the future of Anheuser-Busch and profited greatly.

EF Of course, there were several other stakeholders besides the shareholders who were affected, for example, employees and suppliers. It's beyond doubt that globalisation has led to the loss of jobs through massive rationalisation and cost-cutting measures because profits needed to be hiked in order to at least partially recoup the outlay of the acquisition. Furthermore, it is also beyond doubt that suppliers suddenly found themselves faced with much bigger corporations, who then put pressure on those suppliers with regard to prices and terms of payment. Nonetheless, many suppliers have bulked up in the course of globalisation.

Predator or prey

MS The Beer Monopoly seems to suggest that the players were in a constant crisis mode. How did they handle this?

IV Crisis mode means being in a permanent state of alarm for various reasons. For example, it must have been nerve-racking for Anheuser-Busch's top brass to watch InBev encroach upon them. Carlsberg experienced a crisis when they feared ending up with a new partner in Russia after the possible sale of S&N. Heineken would have had its own crisis when ThaiBev wanted to take over F&N. Alternatively, companies would have been in a state if they did not receive an early warning prior to a sale so they could take the necessary measures. In essence, brewers found themselves in a permanent crisis mode, both internally and externally. Not least, internally when it came to freeing up funds for deals: How much will it cost? How shall we finance it? How high can we go? Will all of our shareholders agree? Such times call for strong leadership and SABMiller's was certainly exemplary in this regard.

MS How did the executive suite manage the expectations of financial markets? Mr Faltermeier, would you also agree with the idea that crisis mode was the normal state of affairs in the game of Beer Monopoly?

EF We have to understand one thing here: the global players we are now discussing did not achieve their status by accident. Instead, they decided early on to actively play the role of buyer and not become a takeover target – predator rather than prey. As such they must constantly maintain a state of high alert, ready to react immediately to everything going on around them. Otherwise they will be evicted from the buyers' camp. Just like the hunters, who hesitate when the wolf turns on them, they will become the hunted.

IV SABMiller comes to mind.

EF This explains the crisis mode. It has nothing to do with living in a constant state of fear that everything will be lost. But it's true, all listed brewers who took a moment to gather their wits and catch their breath in Beer Monopoly quickly found themselves the target of a takeover bid.

MS Hunter or hunted?

EF Yes. This includes communicating what you want to be to the outside world. Only companies with a high market capitalisation can live up to the expectations of the financial markets. Share prices are not necessarily a reflection of the substance of a company, but rather the expectation of what management will do with it. In this sense, expectation management by companies always entails keeping the fantasy alive, so that they can continue to play the role of hunter. Under no circumstances will they allow doubt to arise that the tables could turn.

MS But aside from hunters and hunted, there are other types of player in this world. Will they be able to simply continue to exist as they have in the past?

IV Absolutely. This is particularly applicable to the truly independent companies, those that are still family-owned and -operated. They are not bound to justify and defend every decision to their shareholders. They are free to continue running their businesses just as they have done in the past in spite of globalisation. Take German brewers as an example. Not everyone who doesn't follow the 'buy and build' strategy automatically becomes prey.

MS The general perception of globalisation is that it's all about doing lunch or being lunch. But aren't there also risks associated with the sheer size of a company? We spoke earlier about the possible end of globalisation through a new wave of protectionism. How does that affect a global company?

IV One should never underestimate the influence of politics. This is now evident in Russia, for example. Beer consumption would have never fallen so dramatically had the government not intervened by increasing taxes, prohibiting advertising and limiting the sale of alcohol. In globalisation, politics and governments are major forces to be reckoned with.

MS What other risks are posed purely by the size of the company?

EF Let's look at size on a national scale rather than on a global scale. Imagine a brewer who had elected to focus exclusively on Russia and been very successful there until 2009 when the new regulations came into effect. It would have suffered greatly because its risk are 100 percent dependent on this market. By contrast, a global corporation, which is active on several continents, can better compensate for risks associated with individual markets. A global player can manage individual risks more easily and launch a controlled exit from shaky markets without putting excessive strain on the corporation as a whole. Obviously, in Beer Monopoly it is up to the individual company to create its own risk profile. If today AB-InBev/SABMiller and Heineken have a more favourable risk profile in Russia and China than Carlsberg, which has been badly affected by the decline in both markets, it's because of their wider spread of risks. In this regard, globalisation allowed companies to more cleverly distribute risks and create buffers for worst case scenarios. Naturally, one could always choose the path of greater risk and bigger profits, but the potential to go off the rails was also higher.

MS Would you also consider as risks the expectations of the financial markets?

EF In my opinion, risk always has two sides: it's both the set-up, which is subject to change, and the lead time until the changes actually come into effect. The demands of the financial markets may shift, but it is not something that will impact companies overnight.

They have time to react. Furthermore, any changes in the financial markets will always affect everyone in the industry since they all tap into the same capital markets. Even if there were any tightening in the market, it would still remain a level playing field for all participants.

The next deal is certain

MS The question arises whether it would have been possible to play Beer Monopoly without having to submit to the terms of the institutions providing the financing?

IV The game of Beer Monopoly is only a means to an end, namely to generate new profits from successful deals in order to finance the next deal. It all revolves around the perpetualisation of deals, and the brewing industry has proved to be the best arena for this endeavour.

EF We only need to look to AB-InBev for confirmation of our thesis that Beer Monopoly has been a means to an end. Already the smart money is on the Brazilians to take over another company.

IV The next takeover is as sure as death and taxes, so to speak.

EF And the next deal will not come because Mr Brito is a deal-junkie as the media likes to believe, but rather because the whole finance-led growth model follows this innate law, in a manner of speaking.

MS To what degree is the globalisation of the brewing industry typical of the overall economic globalisation, and which aspects are unique to the brewing industry?

IV I don't believe that the globalisation of the brewing industry can be characterised as typical, especially since it occurred within a relatively short period of time. In the past, there were no truly global brewers on the scale we have now. Anheuser-Busch and Miller may have been leaders in beer once, but that was based on the sheer volume of their sales in the US. Now we have a real market leader, one with a presence in several, very large markets. That's what makes the globalisation of the brewing industry unusual. It happened very quickly and it was made possible thanks to a phenomenon distinctive to the brewing industry.

EF The phenomenon is called national markets. Whoever acquired the respective market leader immediately controlled that market. But only about two dozen of the 40 countries, in which 97 percent of all beer is brewed, possess an attractive profit pool. Those who entered the right countries, like AB-InBev did, could become the biggest and most profitable player in almost no time.

IV The 'buy and build' strategy cannot be applied to other categories in the beverage industry. In the wine industry fragmented markets dominate, whereas the drinks industry revolves around styles, for example, gin, vodka, whisky. In this respect, perhaps the brewing industry really is the exception when it comes to globalisation.

MS How did the game of Beer Monopoly impact beer as a product?

EF Over the past 20 years the global beer market has experienced steady and strong growth, both in terms of volume and purchasing power. This has played a decisive role in supporting the trend toward globalisation. For the most part, beer is not tied to a specific location, except for imported specialties, which consumers regard as high value and aspirational. The terroir of beer, unlike that of wine, is actually meaningless. It's the brand that counts. Furthermore, consumers have a very uniform set of expectations towards beer and this certainly has been reinforced in the past few decades. The differences among the large mainstream brands have levelled out to a large degree – not through a decline in quality but rather by an increase. What some hold against globalisation – that it results in having fewer products to choose from – has also been a boon for product quality overall. This makes products, brands and producers interchangeable, but also opens up new niche markets.

The craft beer phenomenon

MS Now we come to craft beer, an influence originally unforeseen in the game of Beer Monopoly.

EF The rise of craft beer is governed by a simple economic rule that has been proven empirically quite often. The rule says that in consolidated markets with very few players, inevitably a countermovement will occur, drawing new entrants into the market.

IV Sorry, but that is one of those economic rules, which does not automatically apply without external influences. We are actually talking about lowering the barriers to entry. In the US, we would never have witnessed the rise of craft beer had President Carter not legalised homebrewing in 1978. Prior to that, homebrewing was a punishable offence. Furthermore, brewpubs first had to be legalised in the individual states as well – starting in the early 1980s – in order for homebrewers to even contemplate brewing commercially.

EF Nevertheless, craft beer has evolved to become a real challenge for the big brewers – first in the US and then in other countries – where local craft brewers established new breweries, inspired by advances in the US market.

IV We have chosen the term 'disrupter' for craft beer in our model. Since craft beer has taken market share away from the big brewers in their key markets, we find 'disrupter' is an apt descriptor and fits well into our overall picture. We could have gone with the term 'threats' instead, as it commonly appears in strategic SWOT analyses (Strengths, Weaknesses, Opportunities, Threats).

EF External influences are grouped under 'Threats' in SWOT analyses. 'Strengths' and 'Weaknesses' are based on the capabilities of businesses: Can they do the maths, 1+1=3, or not? The perception of craft beer among the big brewers is also of interest: Does it represent a threat or an opportunity? Do the big brewers have the nous to actively play a role in the craft segment, or is craft beer a veritable Achilles heel for the business concept of the big brewers?

IV Actually, it depends on whether you have a couple of hundred million dollars to put on the table to acquire craft brewers, just as AB-InBev has done. Then, craft beer is an opportunity to either expand your own super-premium portfolio or regain lost market share.

EF Correct. For those who don't have the money, craft beer is a threat. For others, it is an opportunity to continue 'buy and build'.

MS Did the big brewers see the rise of craft breweries coming? Could they have predicted or planned for consumer behaviour? Or did it take them completely by surprise?

EF If they had been smart, they would have been actively monitoring the market. It needs to be said that the big brewers have tried to launch products similar to craft beer, known as 'crafty' in the industry. For example, MillerCoors has Blue Moon, AB-InBev introduced Shock Top, while Heineken's contribution is Desperados, and Carlsberg has Jacobsen and Duckstein in its portfolio.

IV However, when you consider that it took Coors 20 years until sales of Blue Moon reached the 2 million hl mark, you realise that this process is too slow for a finance-led brewer. Hence, it's best to stick with 'buy and build'.

EF I object, your honour. We talk far too much about volumes and hectolitres and too little about turnover and profit margins. It's the super-premium positioning of craft beers that makes them attractive.

Real people, real faces

MS Does anyone really know what craft beer is? There are lots of definitions out there, mainly revolving around size, ingredients and ownership.

IV They are far too formulaic in my opinion.

EF In contrast to the big brewers, craft beer is defined by its identification with a location, a company and an owner. Craft brewers have real personalities, not what the big brewers call 'brand personalities'. They have real people with real faces behind the product. And they have myriads of stories. Craft beer has soul – at least this is what consumers see in it.

MS Isn't craft brewers' *raison d'être* and their approach to entrepreneurship fundamentally different from that of the big brewers? Everything revolves around money at AB-InBev, around returns and growth, lowering debt and keeping their shareholders happy. The beer plays a secondary role.

IV Steve Hindy, the founder of the Brooklyn Brewery once said, "Beer comes first, money later." The product is once again at the centre and is no longer viewed as a commodity. Although this philosophy goes against the grain of economic theory, the Brooklyn Brewery is nevertheless a very successful company.

EF In this respect, the statement made by Jim Koch of the Boston Beer Company, that craft beer is "better beer", hits the nail squarely on the head. Not only do craft brewers produce different beers, they also take a different approach to business. At least, this is the impression consumers have.

MS Are craft brewers not casting doubt on the entire deterministic model of growth followed by corporations? That is, that growth is always synonymous with cutting costs?

EF Craft brewers have demonstrated that it is possible to achieve growth and to simultaneously create jobs. According to figures released by the Brewers Association, craft brewers in the US have created a total of 424,000 jobs with more than 115,000 of these jobs directly in breweries and brewpubs.

IV From the perspective of the big brewers, craft brewers are not only cultural 'disrupters'; they also represent a danger to their business. The small brewers are like guerrilla fighters. They siphon off profits from the big brewers' profit pool. In 2016 already, craft brewers control 26 million hl or 14 percent of the US beer market. The proportion of the US beer profit pool going to craft brewers must be far higher.

MS The large number of craft brewery acquisitions made by AB-InBev, MillerCoors, Heineken and Constellation Brands, particularly in 2015, has elicited widespread outrage among craft beer fans.

IV These deals proved to be extremely lucrative for craft brewers willing to sell. SABMiller paid $180 million for Meantime (60,000 hl), with Heineken purchasing half of Lagunitas for perhaps $500 million (900,000 hl) and Constellation parting with $1 billion for Ballast Point (300,000 hl).

EF The deals between the big brewers and the craft brewers are not fuelled by fantasies of share price hikes. Instead, they are governed by a different market logic: brands and consumer demand. I dare say consumers are now riding herd on producers.

MS Aren't the deals a tacit admission by the big brewers that they cannot always meet changing consumer demands with their own recipes?

EF ... and in turn, the craft brewers would have also known that their concept will only work up to a certain point, in terms of size and market share. Perhaps they just lacked the self-confidence of Jim Koch to explore the limits of their growth?

IV These deals should not have caught us unawares, really. Craft brewers must plan for succession. None of the established craft brewers wants to run their brewery until the day they die. European culture requires that children must one day take over the family business, which may explain why so many of the breweries here have been in the family for generations.

EF Family succession does not seem to be very widespread in the US given its cult of the entrepreneur. Also, as a matter of fact, you can only get the full value out of your company when you sell it. Prior to that, you have to live from the profits, provided there are any.

IV What I find interesting about the numerous craft brewery acquisitions made by AB-InBev in 2015 is that they followed in rapid succession. Obviously AB-InBev knew that they would have to complete their expansion into the craft beer segment before embarking on the

SABMiller deal. As part of the settlement with the Department of Justice, each acquisition in the US must now be approved by the anti-trust authorities.

EF I don't think that the anti-trust people will be able to halt future acquisitions of craft breweries, but they could slow them down.

Thanks to the little guys

MS And what does the future hold for craft beer? Many craft brewers are afraid that AB-InBev will undercut them by selling their recently acquired craft beer brands at lower prices.

IV To date, craft brewers have had every reason to thank AB-InBev because AB-InBev's premiumisation strategy has meant they have increased beer prices across the board and did not engage the craft brewers in price wars.

EF The appreciation should be mutual. The big brewers also have a lot to thank the little guys for. They have made their Fast Moving Consumer Goods business sexy again. Perhaps we will see several craft beers previously in the super-premium category now becoming national premium brands, leaving only a few craft beers to defend their super-premium positioning across the nation. Retailers, especially in Europe, tend to push successful and expensive brands down into lower price segments, in order to earn more through higher volumes. I fear that this is a danger for many of the craft beer brands that have been bought by multinational corporations.

MS In the meantime, large American craft brewers have been promoting their brands in foreign markets, either through direct export or by building production breweries in other countries. Just look at what the Brooklyn Brewery did in Scandinavia or the California-based Stone Brewing Co. in Berlin. Does craft going global pose a threat to craft beer itself?

EF I don't see that as a danger, because there are still real people behind the brands and not just avatars. For example, Greg Koch is at Stone, Tony Magee at Lagunitas, Garrett Oliver at Brooklyn Brewery, to name a few. It just so happens that communication is taking place virtually on social media. If you want to follow these guys, you can have a constant feed of their posts and tweets on your devices. It doesn't matter if you are in Singapore or in Seattle. For young people, social media is reality. And the individual, the brewer, remains on stage in the limelight.

IV Perhaps for younger consumers, social media is more important than the other 'real' reality, which has a delivery person bring pizza and beer to their doorstep. And let's not forget the so-called gypsy brewers, such as the Dane Mikkel Borg Bjergsø, better known as Mikkeller, who has forged a new set of rules for globalisation through collaborative brewing. The key phrase is: the sharing economy.

EF I agree, collaborative brewing is different from contract brewing. In the case of contract brewing you have a fictitious brewer appearing on an anonymous beer. In the case of collaboration brews you have two known breweries working together. Collaboration volumes may be small. Nevertheless, this new model offers a way out for the old logistical problem of overcoming geographical distance.

IV Either because of craft beer or thanks to craft beer, the brewing industry is now at a crossroads. In terms of globalisation, the big brewers are going one way and craft brewers the other. In fact, craft brewers are reinventing the rules of globalisation for themselves. That is really what makes it all so exciting.

How will it all play out?

MS How can AB-InBev pay back its debt?

EF Who cares about debt? As long as the fantasy of growth persists, debt is neither a nuisance nor a lasting burden, especially with current low interest rates and brewers' high cash flows.

MS Are there new streets to buy outside of the game of Beer Monopoly? The suffix in the AB-InBev name is 'Bev' and not 'Brew' as it was in 'Interbrew'. Is that a sign?

EF I am assuming that AB-InBev will continue to build its empire, even if it means moving to another industry. We have seen in other industrial sectors that the rules of the game can be rewritten in the quest for growth. As we said before, there is no end to the story.

MS Already AB-InBev has switched teams with the SABMiller deal. It has left the brewing industry to join the consumer goods industry (FMCG). How will this impact their business?

EF Now things are really going to get interesting. Business in this sector is governed by other rules and key performance indicators (KPIs). For brewers, the former KPI of market share was based on beer volumes sold in a certain market. But now Brezhnev's quantitative tons ideology of 'more is better' has been rendered obsolete. The new performance indicators are turnover, return on investment and stock market capitalisation.

IV These are the new overall targets. Otherwise, the companies in this group cannot be compared with one another. It would be like pitting the number of six packs sold against packages of Nespresso capsules or drums of washing powder.

EF Precisely. If you look at the ranking of the FMCG companies, it will become obvious that AB-InBev's dealmaking and strict austerity measures were logical. Of all the companies in the consumer goods industry, brewers have only ever made it to mid-field. Now AB-InBev must show that they can increase turnover, which did not always happen organically in the past.

MS How can brewers continue to grow?

EF This will be difficult to achieve quantitatively. More and more beer markets are becoming saturated, meaning volume growth is stagnant. Therefore, brewers will have to switch to premiumisation and super-premium brands. They will have to make the shift from quantity to quality in an economic sense. But to do so they will need international brands which suggest exclusivity alongside local speciality products, such as craft beers, already in existence. Only then will it be possible to increase turnover and profits without expanding volumes.

IV The 'international premium segment', which comprises the large global beer brands, is still miniscule when considered in terms of world market share. It represents just 6 percent of the volume of beer produced around the world. Local mainstream brands and premium brands still dominate, because overall brewers made more money in these segments.

EF There is still a huge potential for growth with the right brands. And to be honest, only one name comes to mind, and that's Heineken.

MS Has the roadmap for the Beer Monopoly run its course?

IV As for the future, I can only quote the writer Bertolt Brecht, who said: The play is nearly over; the curtain has closed – certainly on SABMiller – but we have so many questions that have yet to be answered. Invariably, the curtain must open again and we will be in for a lot of surprises in the next act.

REFERENCES

Introduction

1 Hansmaennel, Germain. "Weltweite Biergeschäfte." *Lebensmittelzeitung Getränke Spezial.* 2/2006. p. 10. Print.

2 Steiner, Rupert. "Race for Africa: World's biggest brewers battle for control of last untapped market." *thisismoney.co.uk.* 20 August 2013. Web.

3 Gregory, Ross. *Cold War America 1946 to 1990.* New York: Infobase Publishing, 2003. p. 79. Print.

4 AB-InBev. "Our Strategy." Web.

5 Watt, James. *Business For Punks. Break All The Rules – The BrewDog Way.* London: Portfolio Penguin, 2015. p. 51. Print.

Beer goes global

1 MacIntosh, Julie. *Dethroning the King. The Hostile Takeover of Anheuser Busch, an American Icon.* New Jersey: Wiley & Sons, 2011. Print.

2 "Farewell to Scottish & Newcastle." *Spectator.* 6 February 2008. Web.

3 Carlsberg Group. "Heritage." Web.

4 Bjorgolfsson, Bjorgolfur Thor. *Billions to Bust and Back: How I Made, Lost and Rebuilt a Fortune.* London: Profile Books, 2015. p. 2. Print.

5 Griffiths, Ian. "Next-generation Viking invasion." *Guardian.* 16 June 2005. Web.

6 Svennevig, Jan and Isaksson, Maria. "Communication Strategies in a Joint Venture between the Nordic and the Post-Soviet Countries." Dahl, Øyvind, Jensen, Iben and Nynäs, Peter (eds). *Bridges of Understanding. Perspectives on Intercultural Communication.* Oslo: Oslo Academic Press, 2006. p. 213–226. Web.

7 Cope, Nigel. "S&N gulps Hartwall and moves into Russia." *Independent.* 15 February 2002. Web.

8 "South Africa: National Antitrust Laws Are Often Not Enough." *Business Day.* 20 October 2010. Web.

9 Gelles, David. "The Brazilians Behind the Consolidation in Beer." *New York Times.* 16 September 2015. Web.

10 "Beer in China." *Facts and Details.* January 2013. Web.

11 "SABMiller CEO's successor to get less boost from deals." *Reuters.* 20 February 2013. Web.

12 "SAB plan doctored into hostile bid." *fin24.com.* 30 November 2001.Web.

13 Riepl, Wolfgang. *De Belgische bierbaronnen. Het verhaal achter Anheuser-Busch InBev.* Roeselare: Trends Publisher, 2010. p. 212. Print.

14 "Get the beers in." *Week in China.* 22 November 2013. Web.

15 Exane BNP Paribas. "Deal Detox." 11 March 2015. p. 3. Web.

16 MacIntosh, op. cit., p. 120.

17 Eckhardt, Fred. "Anheuser-Busch, gone home." *Potable Curmudgeon (1997).* 28 June 2006. Web.
18 "Marketing: Assess Anheuser-Busch's effort to reach an agreement with the Czechs." *Brainmass.* Web.

AB-InBev: The greatest roll-up in history

1 Munshi, Neil and Daneshkhu, Scheherazade. "Coca-Cola: When less is more." *Financial Times.* 20 April 2015. Web.
2 Daniel Kahneman won the Nobel Prize in Economics in 2002.
3 "Serial thrillers: The agonies and ecstasies of firms that are addicted to doing takeovers." *Economist.* 19 December 2015. Web.
4 "Interbrew, AmBev to Form Brewing Giant." *Washington Post.* 3 March 2004. Web.
5 "Interbrew to acquire Brazil's AmBev." *NBC News.* 3 March 2004. Web.
6 "Will Byers spill Belgian beer?" *Observer.* 3 December 2000. Web.
7 "Brewer Mines Continent's Thirst for Liquid Gold." *Los Angeles Times.* 25 January 1996. Web.
8 Decloet, Derek. "Labatt's Blues." *Globe and Mail.* 30 September 2005. Web.
9 Farnsworth, Clyde. "Labatt Accepts $2.9 Billion Bid From Large Brewer in Belgium." *New York Times.* 7 June 1995. Web.
10 Bilefsky, Dan. "Interbrew Aims to Boost Its Profits By Elevating Stella to the Top Shelf." *Wall Street Journal.* 12 April 2002. Web.
11 Allen, James. "The Beliefs that Built a Global Brewer." *Harvard Business Review.* 27 April 2012. Web.
12 Decloet, Derek. "At Labatt, they miss the Belgians." *Globe and Mail.* 15 September 2006. Web.
13 Walsh, Conan. "Belgian lager mentality." *Guardian.* 4 August 2002. Web.
14 MacIntosh, op. cit., p. 119.
15 Cuadros, Alex. *Brazillionaires: Wealth, Power, Decadence, And Hope in an American Country.* New York: Spiegel & Grau, 2016. p. 197. Print.
16 ibid.
17 Sull, Donald Norman and Escobari, Martin. *Success against the Odds: What Brazilian champions teach us about thriving in unpredictable markets.* Rio de Janeiro: Elsevier/ Campus, 2005. p. 75-96. Print.
18 ibid.
19 Cuadros, op. cit., p. 196.
20 Hill, Andrew and Daneshkhu, Scheherazade. "AB InBev's hard-nosed king of beers." *Financial Times.* 15 June 2015. Web.
21 Sull and Escobari, op. cit.
22 Cuadros, op. cit., p. 201.

23 ibid., p.199.
24 Reguly, Eric. "Bud alert: Brazilians Not all Sunshine and Fun." *Globe and Mail.* 30 June 2008. Web.
25 Callaghan, Shaun, Hawke, Kyle, and Mignerey, Carey. "Five myths (and realities) about zero-based budgeting." *McKinsey & Company.* October 2014. Web.
26 ibid.
27 Allen, op. cit.
28 "SABMiller hält sich aus dem Übernahmekampf heraus." *Handelsblatt.* 21 June 2008. Web.
29 Cimilluca, Dana and Erstl, Mike. "Stella, Bud – Meet Corona." *Wall Street Journal.* 29 June 2012. Web.
30 Davidson, Adam. "Are We in Danger of a Beer Monopoly?" *New York Times Magazine.* 26 February 2013. Web.
31 Cohen, Tim. "The plan to create the biggest beer company in the world." *Financial Mail.* 15 October 2015. Web.
32 Cuadros, op. cit., p. 210-211.

SABMiller: The Graham Show

1 Crotty, Ann. "Boardroom Tails: Mackay's endgame nears." *Financial Mail.* 24 September 2015. Web.
2 AB-InBev. "Proposal to Build the First Truly Global Beer Company." *PR Newswire.* 7 October 2015. Web.
3 Sulaiman, Philip. "Brewing business success: SAB Miller's Graham Mackay." *Media Club South Africa.* 19 December 2013. Web.
4 Bowers, Simon. "SABMiller chief's pay for year nearly £14m." *Guardian.* 24 June 2013. Web.
5 Sulaiman, op. cit.
6 Williams, David. "Reflecting on a special CEO." *Financial Mail.* 16 January 2014. Web.
7 Buck, Jonathan. "Master Brewer Buys a Round." *Barron's.* 20 October 2012. Web.
8 SAB's website says 1970, the historian Anne Kelk Mager says 1979. Mager, Anne Kelk. *Beer, Sociability, and Masculinity in South Africa.* Bloomington: Indiana University Press, 2010. p. 33. Print.
9 ibid., p. 32-33.
10 ibid.
11 Williams, op. cit.
12 Erasmus, Janine. "SABMiller: global brewing giant." *Media Club South Africa.* 7 April 2008. Web.
13 MacIntosh, op. cit., p. 116.

14 Planting, Sasha. "Graham Mackay: the leopard in the room." *Moneyweb.* 18 December 2013. Web.
15 Williams, op. cit.
16 Lobo, Rita. "Africa's untapped beer market." *World Finance.* 13 January 2016. Web.
17 Kitwe and Onitsha. "The beer frontier." *Economist.* 31 May 2014. Web.
18 Sulaiman, op. cit.
19 *FoodStuff South Africa.* 4 September 2009. Web.
20 Williams, op. cit.
21 Crotty, op. cit.
22 Kapner, Suzanne. "South African Brewer Takes Another Look at Buying Miller." *New York Times.* 4 April 2002. Web.
23 Carter, Adrienne. "Miller Brewing: It's Norman Time." *Bloomberg.* 29 May 2006. Web.
24 Cranston, Stephen. "Unflappable Mackay leaves a giant legacy." *Business Day.* 18 December 2013. Web.
25 "SABMiller Chief Executive, Graham Mackay." *wits.ac.za.* 10 June 2011. Web.
26 Carter, op. cit.
27 MacIntosh, op. cit., p. 137-139.
28 "SABMiller Chief Executive, Graham Mackay." op. cit.
29 "SABMiller PLC – Birra Peroni Transaction." *London Stock Exchange's Regulatory News Service.* 14 May 2003. Web.
30 Sibun, Jonathan. "Grolsch to go global after SAB takeover." *Telegraph.* 20 November 2007. Web.
31 Crotty, Ann. "Heineken revives old battle with SAB." *Business Day.* 24 June 2016. Web.
32 MacIntosh, op. cit., p. 139.
33 Hodgson, Jessica. "SAB Shuffles Deckchairs on the Titanic." *Blogs.wsj.* 23 April 2012. Web.
34 Saabira Chaudhuri, Shayndi Raice and Tripp Mickle. "How AB InBev Won Over SABMiller." *Wall Street Journal.* 14 October 2015. Web.
35 Marlow, Ben. "Will there be a hangover following AB-InBev and SAB Miller mega-merger?" *Telegraph.* 14 November 2015. Web.
36 Buck, Jonathan. "Master Brewer Buys a Round." *Barron's.* 20 October 2012. Web.
37 Cole, Robert. "AB InBev must change spots to make SAB deal work." *blogs.reuters.* 13 October 2015. Web.

Heineken: A family affair

1 Heineken N.V. "Heineken responds to recent press speculation." 14 September 2014. Web.
2 Sellers, Patricia. "Heineken's Charlene de Carvalho: A self-made heiress." *Fortune*. 3 December 2014. Web.
3 Rossingh, Danielle. "Heineken heiress remains a mystery." *BBC*. 26 February 2003. Web.
4 Sellers, op. cit.
5 Historion, Jacobs, Mathieu and Maas, Wim. *The Magic of Heineken*. Heineken NV: Amsterdam, 2001. Print.
6 ibid., p. I.9.
7 Molenaar, Marcel. "The 5 Effective Business Principles of Gerard Heineken (1841-1893)." Web.
8 McDonald-Gibson, Charlotte. "Dutch beer magnate 'was not a true Heineken' despite transforming Dutch brewing company into global brand." *Independent*. 6 February 2014. Web.
9 Smit, Barbara. *The Heineken Story: the remarkably refreshing tale of the beer that conquered the world*. Profile Books: London, 2014. Print.
10 Historion, op.cit., p. 5.7
11 ibid., p. 5.10.
12 ibid., p. 9.35.
13 ibid., p. 9.27.
14 Sellers, op. cit.
15 ibid.
16 Historion, op. cit., p. 12.13.
17 Smit, op. cit., p. 238.
18 ibid., p. 260.
19 Rossingh, op. cit.
20 Sellers, op. cit.
21 Thomas, Nathalie. "Heineken reveals why Tiger deal isn't small beer." *Telegraph*. 8 December 2012. Web.
22 Smit, op. cit., p. 285
23 "Heineken and Diageo swap assets in 3 continents." *Financial Times*. 7 October 2015. Web.

Carlsberg: The lone ranger

1 Carlsberg Group. *Annual Report* 2015. 24 February 2016. p. 14-15. Web.
2 Jes Iversen, Martin and Arnold, Andrew. "Carlsberg: from exporter to an integrated multinational enterprise." *Journal of the Brewery History Society*. Vol 181, 2009. p. 51-62. p. 56. Web.
3 ibid., p. 55.

4 ibid., p. 57.
5 Heller, Richard. "At Sea in an Ocean of Beer."*Forbes.* 30 October 2000. Web.
6 ibid.
7 Verstl, Ina and Hansmaennel, Germain. "Neues Spiel, neues Glück." *Brauwelt Jubiläumsausgabe – 150 Jahre.* 11 August 2011. p. 44-48. Print.
8 "Tesco-Supermärkte werfen Carlsberg raus." *Brauwelt.* Vol 48 (2015). p. 1436. Print.
9 Heller, op. cit.
10 "ORKLA ASA – Company Profile." *Reference for Business.* Web.
11 ibid.
12 ibid.
13 "Orkla and Carlsberg form global beer company." *Hugin.* 31 May 2000. Web.
14 ibid.
15 "ORKLA ASA – Company Profile." *Reference for Business.* Web.
16 Jes Iversen, Martin and Arnold, Andrew, op.cit., p. 60.
17 ibid.
18 "Feldschlösschen verkauft." *Brauwelt.* Vol 23/24 (2000). p. 967. Print.
19 "Carlsberg übernimmt Feldschlösschen Gruppe." *Brauwelt.* Vol 45 (2000). p. 1992. Print.
20 Carlsberg Breweries. "Carlsberg Breweries. Übernahme der Holsten-Brauerei 20. Januar 2000. Conference Call." 20 January 2004. Web.
21 "Carlsberg and Heineken satisfy antitrust conditions for acquisition of Scottish & Newcastle." *GlobeNewswire.* 3 April 2009. Web.
22 "Heineken und Carlsberg kaufen Scottish & Newcastle." *Neue Zürcher Zeitung.* 26 January 2008. Web.
23 Carlsberg Group. "Acquisition of Scottish and Newcastle UK. Creation of the World's Fastest Growing Global Brewer." 10 March 2008. Web.
24 "Heineken und Carlsberg kaufen Scottish & Newcastle." op. cit.
25 Carlsberg Group. "FINAL S&N Offer. Creation of the World's Fastest Growing Global Brewer." 25 January 2008. Web.
26 USDA Foreign Agricultural Service. "Russian Beer Market Update." GAIN Report Number RFATO032. 19 February 2016. p. 4. Web.
27 Milne, Richard. "Carlsberg: Trouble brewing in Russia." *Financial Times.* 27 September 2012. Web.
28 Heller, op. cit.
29 Milne, op. cit.
30 Carlsberg Group. *Annual Report 2015.* 24 February 2016. p. 40. Web.
31 Milne, Richard. "Carlsberg strategy draws flat reception from investors." *Financial Times.* 16 March 2016. Web.
32 "Jorge Paulo Lemann." *Forbes. The World's Billionaires* 2016. Web.
33 "Carlsberg announces its SAIL'22 strategy." *Euroland.* 16 March 2016. Web.

34 ibid.
35 Carlsberg Group. *Annual Report* 2015. p. 9. Web.
36 Kelch, Kai and Hohmann, Christine. "Die größten Brauereigruppen und Privatbrauereien 2015." Brauwelt. Vol 9-10 (2016). p. 256 f. Print.
37 Carlsberg Group. *Annual Report* 2015. p. 9. Carlsberg A/S. Annual Report 2005. 5 March 2006. p. 8. Web.
38 Carlsberg Group. "SAIL '22. Conference Call. Transcript." 16 March 2016. Web.
39 Deutsche Bank Markets Research. "Tapping into growth." 29 July 2014. p. 27. Web.
40 Carlsberg Group. "Acquisition of Scottish and Newcastle UK. Creation of the World's Fastest Growing Global Brewer." 10 March 2008. Web.
41 Carlsberg Group. *Annual Report* 2015. 24 February 2016. p. 55. Web.

CAST OF CHARACTERS

The globalisation of the brewing industry knew many players, all with backstories that frequently entwined. Readers requiring a run-down of Who's Who are advised to consult this list. Our classification does not reflect the companies' economic ranking but their strategic function in the Beer Monopoly.

Main Cast

AB-InBev

The world's number one brewer, formed after the takeover of Anheuser-Busch in 2008. Subsequently it acquired Grupo Modelo and SABMiller. It owns brands like Budweiser, Corona Extra (excluding the US), Stella Artois, Brahma, Skol and Beck's.

SABMiller

The former world's number two brewer with roots in South Africa bought Miller in the US in 2002 to become SABMiller. It owned about 200 brands, including Pilsner Urquell, Miller Lite, Peroni, Grolsch and Castle, and was taken over by AB-InBev in 2015.

Heineken

Ranked global number two brewer, the Dutch family-controlled company embarked on a catch up race in globalisation when it bought BBAG, Bravo, S&N, FEMSA Cerveza and its partner's stake in APB.

Carlsberg

The world's number three brewer with origins in Denmark entered into Russia through the joint venture with Orkla and into China plus Vietnam through the takeover of S&N. It owns more than 170 brands including Carlsberg, Tuborg, Baltika, Kronenbourg and Holsten.

Supporting Cast

Altria

Formerly known as the cigarette maker Philip Morris, it owned the US brewer Miller that was sold to SAB in 2002 for which Altria received a stake in SABMiller.

AmBev

Born from the merger of Brahma and Antarctica, it is the leading brewer in Brazil. It bought Argentina's brewer Quilmes and Canada's Labatt and merged with Interbrew to form InBev. Among its brands are Brahma, Antarctica, and Skol.

Anheuser-Busch

Leading brewer in the US with brands including Budweiser and Bud. It was taken over by InBev in 2008.

Asia Pacific Breweries (APB)

Asian brewer with headquarters in Singapore, it was established by Fraser & Neave and Heineken in 1931. Since 2012 it has been fully owned by Heineken. Its major brand is Tiger Beer.

Baltic Beverages Holding (BBH)

Based in Sweden, it was founded in 1991 by Sweden's brewer Pripps and Finland's Hartwall as a holding company for their brewing activities in the Baltics and Russia. Since 2008 Carlsberg fully controls BBH, thus becoming the largest brewer in eastern Europe with brands like Baltika and Tuborg.

Bavaria

see Santo Domingo

BBAG

Founded in 1988 with breweries in Austria, Hungary, Czech Republic and Romania, this Austrian group later became Brau Union and was sold to Heineken in 2003.

Beck's

Germany's major beer exporter, the family-controlled brewer was among the first to sell to a foreign competitor. It was taken over by Interbrew in 2001.

Bond Corporation

Controlled by Alan Bond, who was later convicted of fraud, it consolidated the Australian beer market and expanded into the US and the UK before going into receivership in 1992. The Australian beer unit was taken over by New Zealand's Lion. Today Lion is owned by Kirin.

Bravo International

Founded by two twenty-something Icelandic adventurers in the 1990s, Bravo became the number four brewer in Russia before it was bought by Heineken in 2003. The founders subsequently became embroiled in the collapse of Iceland's banks.

Brewpole

An executive under Alan Bond, Tony Oates bolted to Poland to set up Brewpole as a holding for various breweries, which were merged to become the leading brewer in Poland. It later combined with Heineken's Zywiec when Mr Oates was extradited to Australia to serve a prison sentence.

Carlsberg Foundation

Managing the legacy of brewers Jacobsen, it holds the majority of voting rights in Carlsberg and a considerable stake in Carlsberg's share capital. The Foundation is mainly funded by Carlsberg's dividends.

CCU

Leading brewer in Chile and jointly controlled by Heineken and Quiñenco since 2003

Cuauhtémoc Moctezuma

see FEMSA Cerveza

Feldschlösschen

Major Swiss brewer which was acquired by Carlsberg in 2000.

FEMSA Cerveza

Number two brewer in Mexico with brands Sol, Tecate, Dos Equis. It was taken over by Heineken in 2010 in exchange for a stake in Heineken.

Foster's

After a failed global expansion in the 1980s, Foster's rose from the ashes and attempted to become a leading international wine and beer company. As the wine unit never delivered, shareholders pushed for a split of the two. The Australian beer unit (CUB) was sold to SABMiller in 2011.

Grupo Modelo

Mexico's number one brewer with brands including Corona Extra and Modelo Especial, in which Anheuser-Busch had a stake. The remaining stake was sold to AB-InBev in 2013.

Holsten

A leading German brewer, stock market-listed but family-controlled. In 2004 it was sold to Carlsberg, which broke it up and sold extraneous units to a German rival.

InBev

The result of the merger between Brazil's AmBev and Belgium's Interbrew in 2004.

Interbrew

The major Belgian brewer with brands like Stella Artois, Leffe, Jupiler and Hoegaarden, which bought Labatt and merged with AmBev to become InBev.

Labatt

Canadian conglomerate which was sold to Interbrew in 1995.

Miller Brewing

The number two brewer in the US which was sold to SAB in 2002 and later entered into a joint venture with the third-largest US brewer Coors to form MillerCoors. Now fully owned by Molson Coors.

Molson Coors

Formed through the 2005 merger of Canada's brewer Molson and US brewer Coors, it is controlled by the Molson and Coors families and has businesses in North America, the UK and central Europe

Orkla

Norwegian conglomerate, whose beer interests including a stake in BBH, were merged with Carlsberg's to form Carlsberg Breweries. The partners fell out with each other and Orkla was bought out by Carlsberg in 2004.

Santo Domingo

Colombian family which controlled the brewer Bavaria, the market leader in Colombia, Peru and Ecuador. It sold Bavaria in exchange for a stake in SABMiller in 2005.

Scottish & Newcastle (S&N)

Major UK brewer which prettied itself up for a sale by taking over France's Kronenbourg, Finland's Hartwall (BBH) and various other participations. It was jointly taken over by Carlsberg and Heineken in 2008

United Breweries (UB)

Inherited by the colourful Indian liquor baron VJ Mallya, it became the leading brewer in India. Mr Mallya struck a deal with S&N in 2004, whose stake in UB ended up with Heineken in 2008.

Van Munching

Exclusive importer of Heineken beer in the US until 1991 when Heineken took it over.

Minor Cast

Asahi

The market leader in Japan, which bought Italy's Peroni and Dutch Grolsch from SABMiller in 2016. It has a minority stake in Chinese brewer Tsingtao.

Castel Group

Owned by the Castel family, the French company is the largest wine producer in Europe and vies with Heineken for the title of number two brewer in Africa. It has a cross shareholding with SABMiller.

Constellation Brands

The US drinks group obtained the rights to Corona Extra and other Modelo brands in the US in perpetuity when AB-InBev took over Grupo Modelo in 2013. It ranks as number three brewer in the US.

China Resources Snow

Variously called CR Snow, CR Enterprises or CR Breweries, it is the leading brewer in China. SABMiller's 49 percent stake was bought back by CR Beer in 2016.

Diageo

One of the world's leading drinks companies, it has brands like Smirnoff, Johnnie Walker, and Guinness in its portfolio. It also owns the Guinness beer company based in Ireland.

Efes

Also known as Anadolu Efes, the Turkey-based company is a Coca-Cola bottler in mainly Muslim countries and a beer producer in Moldova, Ukraine, Georgia, Russia and Kazakhstan. It is an associate of SABMiller.

Kirin

The number two brewer in Japan owns brewers in Australia, New Zealand (Lion) as well as Brazil (Schincariol) and has a stake in Philippine brewer San Miguel.

INDEX

ABOUT THE AUTHORS

Having closely followed and written about the brewing industry for many years, two economists, Dr Ina Verstl and Ernst Faltermeier, have here provided a timely analysis of globalisation as the industry reaches a pivotal moment in its history.

For nearly two decades Dr Verstl has been a business correspondent for Brauwelt International, a leading and long-established independent publication focusing on the world of beer. Born in Germany, she grew up in England. After studying economics, philosophy and literature in Munich, Hull and Oxford, she gained a doctorate at the University of Zurich. Her blog is beermonopoly.net.

Following his Masters degrees in brewing and economics at the Technical University of Munich, Ernst Faltermeier held executive positions with large international and German brewing companies before joining the management board of one of Germany's major beer and beverage distributors, Nordmann. He is now sharing his expertise as strategy consultant, board member and lecturer in Management and Finance in Hamburg.